MASTERING
THE BUSINESS OF ORGANIZING

A Guide to Plan, Launch, Manage, Grow, and Leverage a Profitable, Professional Organizing Business

2nd ed., revised

Anne M. Blumer, CPO®

Copyright © 2018 Anne M. Blumer, CPO.

5 Steps to Organizing® is a registered trademark of SolutionsForYou, Inc.

All rights reserved. No part of this book may be reproduced, stored, or transmitted by any means—whether auditory, graphic, mechanical, or electronic—without written permission of the author, except in the case of brief excerpts used in critical articles and reviews. Unauthorized reproduction of any part of this work is illegal and is punishable by law.

ISBN: 978-1-4834-9808-9 (sc)
ISBN: 978-1-4834-9537-8 (e)

Library of Congress Control Number: 2018911789

Because of the dynamic nature of the Internet, any web addresses or links contained in this book may have changed since publication and may no longer be valid. The views expressed in this work are solely those of the author and do not necessarily reflect the views of the publisher, and the publisher hereby disclaims any responsibility for them.

This book is a work of non-fiction. Unless otherwise noted, the author and the publisher make no explicit guarantees as to the accuracy of the information contained in this book and in some cases, names of people and places have been altered to protect their privacy.

Any people depicted in stock imagery provided by Getty Images are models, and such images are being used for illustrative purposes only.
Certain stock imagery © Getty Images.

Lulu Publishing Services rev. date: 02/07/2019

Other Books by Anne M. Blumer, CPO

1. Get Rich Organizing
   The Professional Organizer Survival Guide to Launch, Manage, and Grow a Profitable Business
2. Get Organized TODAY

Praise for *Mastering the Business of Organizing—A Guide to Plan, Launch, Manage, Grow, and Leverage a Profitable, Professional Organizing Business*

This book is mighty. Anne is the true expert in transferring the skills, framework, and plan for your organizing career. Her methodology and training led me to confidently launch my company, Simplify Experts, and build it into a thriving, multiple six-figure revenue stream. Follow her plan!

—Denise Allan, CPO-CD, CPO
Simplify Experts, LLC
Author of *Declutter and Thrive*

Mastering the Business of Organizing is a "how-to" masterpiece! In my twenty-four-plus years as a professional organizer, there has never been anything quite like it. Here, Anne generously shares her wisdom and knowledge from her fifteen years' experience in the organizing field. Each chapter is sequentially organized and is a complete compilation of easy-to-read instructions and concepts with all the tools necessary for starting, running, managing, and marketing a professional organizing business. A fabulous must-have for anyone interested in enhancing, advancing, or exploring the field of professional organizing.

—Sheila Delson, CPO-CD, CPO
Freedom Domain Concepts
www.freedomainconcepts.com

I am extremely organized in my own home and love every bit of the organizing process. I had considered starting my own business for a long time but always dismissed the thought because I didn't think I could be successful. I ordered Anne Blumer's *Mastering the Business of Organizing* before signing up for her Institute for Professional Organizers, Self- Study Education program and Seminar/Client Practicum. The book is filled with valuable information for anyone trying to start their own professional organizing business. Anne provides great detail to the entire business process. There is the beginning basics, start-up information, the organizing process, working with clients, and how to keep your business running. I learned so much from Anne Blumer and also gained experience, which gave me the confidence to start my own business.

Mastering the Business of Organizing continues to be a great guide to me in my business endeavors.

—Suzanne Redpath,
Professional Organizer
A&E Organizing, LLC

Mastering the Business of Organizing is a comprehensive resource for professional organizers. Prospective and new organizers will learn both what steps to take to set up a smooth-running business and the breadth of skills they will want to cultivate to succeed in helping the variety of clients they will encounter. Veteran organizers will glean plenty of ideas to help them grow and evolve their businesses. This book is a valuable asset for every professional organizer's library.

—Valentina Sgro
ReallyOrganized.com
Past president of the Institute for Challenging Disorganization
Award-winning author of the *Patience Oaktree* organizing novels and short stories

To my husband, Stefan. Without you, I never would have launched my professional organizing business, SolutionsForYou, Inc. Your constant loving support, sacrifices, and encouragement gave me the space and time to write *Mastering the Business of Organizing.* You have been my inspiration and my anchor.

To my children, Alex and Hannah, I am tremendously blessed and grateful you are in my life. You were the reason I wanted flexibility in my career, so I could be there when you needed me. I hope I always was and continue to be.

And to my dog, Brinkley, who kept my feet warm and anchored at my computer while I wrote *Mastering the Business of Organizing* and whose loyal and quiet companionship is missed every day.

CONTENTS

Foreword by Ingrid Jansen, Organise Your House xvii

Acknowledgments xix

Preface—My Journey and How I Grew My Organizing Business with Multiple
    Streams of Revenue xxi

Introduction xxxv

Part I   The Business of Organizing

Chapter 1   Introduction to Professional Organizing 1

Professional Organizer Definition 1
Getting Started in the Professional Organizing Business 2
Characteristics 3
Top Ten Considerations in Becoming a Professional Organizer 5
NAPO History and Overview 6
National Membership 6
Chapter Membership 7
Professional Organizer Specialties 7
NAPO Code of Ethics 8
Certification 9
Additional Industry Associations 10
✍ Exercises 10
📄 Actions 11

Chapter 2   Assessing Your Skills 12

What Are Your Strengths? 12
What Is Your Background? 13
What Is Your Job Experience? 13
A Typical Day for a Professional Organizer 13

A Typical Day for a Business Owner...15
Training and Education..15
Working with Clients Training and Education..15
Small Business Training and Education 16
✎ Exercises...17

Chapter 3   Writing a Business Plan...18

Questions to Ask Before Writing Your Business Plan...19
Business Concept..19
Mission Statement..19
Market and Customer Analysis 20
Strategy..20
Opportunities (Problems and Opportunities) 20
Products and Services..21
Competition 21
Niche...21
Goals and Objectives 21
Financial Plan 22
Action Plan for Getting Started 23
Resource Requirements..25
Key Issues..25
Risks (Threats) and Rewards 25
SWOT Analysis 25
📄 Actions 28

Chapter 4   Fee Structures—How to Charge for Your Services..........................29

Selling Your Value 29
How to Describe the Benefits (Value) Your Client Will Receive 30
Hourly Fee versus Project Fee...30
Packages 31
Initial Consultation and Needs Assessment...31
Travel Fee 32
Materials Fee..32
National Average 32
Articles Quoting Professional Organizer Fees 32
How to Determine Your Fee 33
When and How to Give Yourself a Raise 33
Final Word on Fees 34
📄 Actions 34

Chapter 5	Business Basics	35
	Office Basics Checklist	35
	Field Materials Checklist	37
	📄 Actions	39
Chapter 6	Determine Legal and Insurance Needs	40
	Registering with State and Federal Governments	40
	Insurance	41
	Permits and Licensing	41
	What Goes into Selecting Your Choice of Business Entity?	41
	Sole Proprietorship	42
	General Partnership	42
	Corporation	43
	S Corporation	44
	Limited Liability Company (LLC)	44
	📄 Actions	46
Chapter 7	Name and Register Your Business for Maximum Impact	47
	What's in a Name?	47
	What Do You Want to Project?	47
	First Impressions Do Matter	47
	Be Careful Using Your Own Personal Name	48
	Choose Your Name Wisely	49
	Register Your Business Name	49
	📄 Actions	50
Chapter 8	Tax Issues to Consider and Understand: What You Need to Know to Be Tax Savvy and Tax Benefits You Should Understand	51
	Software Options for Your Business Records	51
	Tips on Setting up Quicken or QuickBooks	52
	Deductions for Your Business	52
	Business Use of Home	53
	Business Use of Automobile	55
	Business Travel	55
	Business versus Personal Travel Expenses	56
	Estimated Taxes	56
	Payroll Taxes	57
	📄 Actions	58

Chapter 9 Marketing and Branding Your Organizing Business and How to Find Clients .. 59

What Is the Difference between Marketing, Advertising, and Public Relations? 59
Creating Your Brand 60
Writing a Winning Marketing Message and Communicating Your Value 60
Creating Your Elevator Speech 62
How to Find Clients 63
Developing Your Network of Strategic Alliances..63
Developing a Successful Website 64
Five Steps to Creating a Blog with Google 66
Thirty-Minute Marketing Formula 66
Top Ten Marketing Approaches..67
One Hundred Marketing Approaches 68
First-Year Marketing Plan 72
📄 Actions 73

Part II The Client Process

Chapter 10 Client Process —Phase 1: Connecting with the Client 77

Client Process..77
Points to Consider to Prepare You for When Your Client Calls 78
The First Five Questions to Ask 78
Developing Your Thirty-Second Hook 78
What You Need to Know from Your Client—Closing the Conversation.....................79
You Have a Consultation Scheduled—What's Next? 80
Preparing for the Needs Assessment..80
Checklists 81
✎ Exercises..81

Chapter 11 Client Process—Phase 2: How to Effectively Conduct a Needs Assessment and Scheduling the Project...82

Overview..82
What to Expect..83
Conducting the Needs Assessment..84
Scheduling the Project 86
Services and Fees Agreement 86
Job Agreement Components (See the Forms Section in Appendix A for an Example of a Services and Fees Letter of Agreement)..87
Other Business Policies to Consider and Communicate 90
📄 Actions 91

Chapter 12 Client Process—Phase 3: Completing the Client Project with the 5 Steps to Organizing® Process 92

Organizing Plan of Action 92
Organizing Plan of Action—Example 93
5 Steps to Organizing 98
Step 1— Strategize 99
Step 2—Prioritize 99
Keep-Let Go Criteria 100
Stumbling Block Excuses 102
Step 3—Localize 103
Step 4—Containerize 104
Step 5—Maximize 104
Ten Organizing Principles 105
✎ Exercises 106

Chapter 13 Client Follow-Up: Prevent Backsliding 107

Thank-You Note 107
Sample Thank-You Note 107
Maintenance Plan 108
Maintenance Plan Template 108
Follow-Up Appointment 109
Client Satisfaction Survey 109
📄 Actions 110

Part III Working with Clients

Chapter 14 Safety for Professional Organizers and Their Clients 113

Hazards 114
Safety Points 118
Your Client's Safety 119
Personal Protective Gear 119

Chapter 15 The Challenging Clients You Will Meet 121

Case Studies 121
Angela—Clients with Attention Deficit Disorder (ADHD) 122
Trudy—Chronically Disorganized Clients 126
Mary—Clients Who Hoard 129
Priscilla— Senior Clients 132

Chapter 16   Working with Clients on Paper Management 135

Benefits of Organizing Your Paper Information 135
The ART of Paper Management 136
Paper Information Organizational Chart 137
Create a Paper-Processing Center 137
Where to Start 138
File Strategies 138
What to Keep and How Long 139
How and Where to Keep the Paper Management System 139
Products/Systems for Your Reference Papers—Tax Records 140
Products/Systems for Tracking Your Finances 140
Products/Systems for Digital Financial Records 141
Maintenance—The Key 141
   📄 Actions 142

Chapter 17   Working with Clients on Time Management 143

Where Are You Spending Your Time? 143
What Causes Procrastination? 144
Planning Your Time 145
Time-Management Tools 146
   📄 Actions 147

Chapter 18   Working with Clients on Clutter Control 148

What Is Clutter? 148
Why Does Clutter Happen? 149
What Is Clutter Costing You? 149
What Are the Benefits of Eliminating Clutter? 149
Why Does Disorganization Happen? 149
Understanding Your Relationship with Your Clutter 150
How to Create a Visual Plan of What You Want Your Space to Look and Feel Like 151
How to Stop Cluttering and Start Organizing 151
   ✍ Exercises 152

In Summary 153

Appendix A: Forms 155

Initial Client Contact Information 155
Onsite Needs Assessment /
   Consultation Preparation Checklist 157
Onsite Needs Assessment /
   Consultation Appointment Checklist 157

Organizing Appointment Checklist 157
Residential Needs Assessment Questionnaire 158
Business Needs Assessment Questionnaire 161
Organizing Plan of Action 165
Floor Plan 168
Example Organizing Company Services and Fees
    Letter of Agreement 169
Time Map / Weekly Plan 172

Appendix B: Recommended Reading 175

Organizing 175
Small Business 176
Time Management and Productivity 176
Organizing Fiction 176

Appendix C: Websites 177

Appendix D: Organizing Products 178

About the Author 179

FOREWORD BY INGRID JANSEN, ORGANISE YOUR HOUSE

Congratulations on buying this book! You've just made a very sound investment in your business and yourself. You either are contemplating starting a career as a professional organizer, have just started out running your own business, have been going for a while now and want to check if you've covered all your bases, or you've been doing this a long time and you just want to cross all the T's and dot all the I's. Whatever reason you might have, reading this book is a smart thing to do! I've read the book cover to cover, and although I've been a professional organizer myself for eight years and am well established, I've definitely got a few things on my to-do list after reading Anne's book. It just shows that you're never too old to learn even if you've been in the profession for a while.

I had the privilege to meet Anne back in 2015 at the APDO conference (the Association of Professional Declutterers and Organisers in the UK) where she delivered the keynote and also ran a breakout session for sixty UK professional organizers. I was completely inspired by Anne's professionalism and knowledge, and we instantly became friends and have been ever since. We stay connected through social media and cheer each other's successes. The fact that my daughter is also called Anne must have helped with our connection. Furthermore, Anne is a lovely and kind person, and I was excited we were able to meet again at the NAPO Pittsburgh conference in 2017.

I'm thrilled and delighted to have been asked to write this foreword, and I encourage you to dive into this book if you're serious about becoming a well-rounded professional organizer. Being a successful organizer is not only being able to connect with your clients and being "good at organizing." It also requires you to be a capable business person. This book serves both purposes, and the key action points at the end of each chapter will focus you on the next steps.

Like Anne, I've volunteered for APDO for six years, first as a conference committee member for two years and then four years as APDO president. Volunteering for your local chapter or on a national level will propel you to knowledge and connections you could not have envisioned.

Good luck on your journey!

My warmest,
Ingrid Jansen
Immediate Past President APDO 2018–2019
President APDO 2014–2018

ACKNOWLEDGMENTS

I want to thank all the participants who have attended a training program with me. I have learned and improved my teaching because of your curiosity, never-ending questions, and brilliant suggestions.

A very special and heartfelt thank you to all my clients who have entrusted me with their fears, anxiety, and personal possessions, with faith that I will guide them to a better way of living.

PREFACE—MY JOURNEY AND HOW I GREW MY ORGANIZING BUSINESS WITH MULTIPLE STREAMS OF REVENUE

The first question people ask me after learning I'm a professional organizer is, "What led you to this career?" I'm going to share my journey and how I have mastered the business of organizing.

Over the years leading up to starting my business, friends and coworkers would comment on my home environment or workspace and tell me I should do "this" for a living. I didn't know what they meant by "this."

One day, someone said, "I would love for you to organize my kitchen." I looked at her like she was crazy, and I thought, *Doesn't everyone have things organized in their kitchen?* I didn't realize that not everyone is organized. I didn't even really think about the word *organized* because I didn't realize that other people didn't know how to be organized—even though two very disorganized parents raised me! However, growing up, I didn't think of my parents as disorganized; I thought of them as messy, forgetful, and late to appointments.

What led me to this career was others noticing a skill—organizing—in me that I wasn't even aware of and the realization that others would want to pay me to help them organize their stuff. I could be paid to do what comes naturally to me and what I *love* to do—organize!

The second question people ask me after learning I'm a professional organizer is, "Have you always been organized, or did you learn organizing skills?" For as long as I can remember, I have been organized with my space and my time. I think I developed organizing skills out of necessity to feel some control over my space and time because my family life as a child was chaotic and unpredictable. Developing structure gave me a sense of control, and that gave me a feeling of calm.

When I was a young child, my favorite thing to do when I would go over to my best friend's house to play was to help her tidy up her room. Her mother loved me! I was constantly rearranging my bedroom furniture, cleaning my room, writing to-do lists, and posting my daily routine. Now that I think about it, my parents were quite lucky to have me as their child.

In 2001, I left my human resources position with a high-technology company I had worked at for thirteen years. I left because I wanted to graduate that June with my degree in organizational communication. To do so, I needed to take more than a full-time course load, which meant I needed to stop working.

I graduated in June, and then in September, my husband, Stefan, and I married. I was in career transition and busy raising two young children. Alex was nine, and Hannah was seven years old. I was searching for what was next because I knew I wanted to be more than a stay-at-home parent. But I also knew I wanted to be there for Alex and Hannah after school as they were growing up, since I had not been able to in their early years.

I would not have started a professional organizing business if it were not for my husband, Stefan.

It was New Year's Eve 2002, and we were sitting at home by a warm fire, watching the snow fall. Stefan turned to me and said, "I want to start a consulting business, and I want to do it tonight!"

My response was, "Can't we just drink wine and sit by the fire like everyone else who doesn't go out on New Year's Eve?"

Stefan said, "You drink. I'm starting a business. And you will be able to do your organizing thing under it too." And by golly he did! He downloaded the state of Oregon's Small Business Guide, and by January 17, 2003, we were incorporated. Keep in mind, Stefan is Swiss!

We named the company SolutionsForYou, Inc. In retrospect, that was the first significant mistake we made. Generically, it works for both of our services because it doesn't say specifically what solutions we provide. But from a marketing standpoint, it is not specific enough because it doesn't have the word *organize* or *organizing* in it. If we were to do it over, I would have formed Blumer Enterprises as the corporation and registered separate DBAs (doing business as) with specific names for our services. From a marketing perspective, your business name needs to say specifically what you do to be searchable on the internet. To remedy this error, I added my tagline "providing effortless solutions to organizing" for web search ability and other marketing needs.

Stefan did the heavy lifting of building the company's infrastructure and the company's website with two separate businesses, his consulting and my organizing.

I wasn't sure how viable a profession organizing was, so I searched "organizing" on the internet. The National Association of Professional Organizers, now National Association of Productivity & Organizing Professionals (NAPO) was at the top of the search list. I clicked on their website and was amazed to learn over 1,200 people were doing this for a profession. I got even more excited to learn there was a local chapter of NAPO in my city. It was January 17, and that was the day I joined both NAPO national and the Oregon chapter. I attended my first meeting the following week. You will learn more about NAPO and other industry associations in chapter 1.

From there, I spent three months working on marketing, website content, bookkeeping, a client records system, leads tracking, and gathering organizing supplies. I discovered how much I love managing a business, especially marketing—something I had no experience or education in.

But what I had not done was write a business plan. I was doing what I thought should be done without any thought as to what *needed* to be done. I'll talk more about this in chapter 3 and what a mistake it was.

I attended NAPO meetings monthly, and within six months, I was asked to serve on the Oregon board as board secretary. I was thrilled that they wanted me and of course said yes! I remained on the Oregon board for seven years and retired as chapter president. This was probably the single most important action I took in my first year of business to develop my skills and education as a professional organizer and to promote my business.

My first piece of advice to you is this: be of service to an industry association and watch what happens to your business and you.

We were four months into the start-up of the business. Stefan and I were in our office with our desks back to back, and he turned around, kicked my chair, and said, "Don't you think it's about time to get a client?"

I had not worked with a client yet. I wasn't even sure how to go about finding clients, and our website was not on page 1 of the search listing, so if anyone was looking for a professional organizer, they would not find me. Remember, this was 2003, and professional organizers were not commonplace. The TV shows that have promoted our industry were just beginning.

I asked Stefan, "How should I go about finding clients?" He suggested I ask a few friends who had encouraged me to do this, to see if they knew of anyone whose home was a bit cluttered. I pulled together a brochure of my business services and proceeded to meet with everyone I knew, asking them to help me find clients.

This exercise proved to be very worthwhile on two counts.

First, I was referred by one of my friends to her client, and I had my first organizing job. Second, I made connections with people who have businesses with clients who need my services, and eventually my clients might need their services. For example, one friend is a financial advisor, and her clients needed help pulling together paper information the financial advisor needed to advise them on. My clients often ask me if I know of a financial advisor because they need to get their finances in order or want to start investing for their retirement. It's a win-win relationship and what is known as a strategic alliance.

If you haven't already formed a group of strategic alliances, think of who they could be (you'll learn more about strategic alliances in chapter 9). Invite them to meet with you, explain your services, and then ask them, "How can I be of service to you?" and watch the flood of referrals come your way. And you will be more valuable to your clients because you have resources for them.

Another way to meet strategic partners is to join networking organizations. Business Networking International is one networking organization I belonged to. They have over 200,000 members. I met many business owners; we exchanged referrals, and I grew my list of trusted resources.

When I started as a professional organizer, I didn't know what I didn't know. I thought I would be putting pretty things in pretty containers and labeling them. I thought I could organize anyone—and in one day!

I worked with my first client in May 2003. Her name is Susie, and a friend who I gave some of my business brochures to referred her to me. I met with Susie, and she gave me a tour of her home. As we went from room to room, I kept thinking to myself, *Why am I here?* The rooms didn't seem disorganized or even terribly cluttered. As we finished the tour inside the home, Susie said, "Now for the garage."

When she opened the door to the garage, I understood why I was there. This was a basic case of situational disorganization. Situational disorganization happens when a precipitating event causes disruption—such as moving, a new job, getting married, parenthood, divorce, serious illness, or the death of a loved one. For Susie, the precipitating event was motherhood. Her time outside of parenting and working full-time was now limited. Susie found the time to declutter her home and move what she was no longer using out to the garage to "deal with later." Later never came, and the piles grew over the years. When Susie and I worked together, she was able to make decisions easily about what to keep and what to finally release. After working with Susie, I hoped all my clients' projects would be like hers.

It wasn't long before I learned that would not be the case and that many of my clients' disorganization had *nothing* to do with their stuff and much more to do with their brain-based challenges. My advice is to have assessment questions that will identify if your client is situationally disorganized or chronically disorganized and what brain-based challenges they have. You'll learn more about needs assessments in chapter 11 and working with the chronically disorganized in chapter 15.

I attended my first NAPO conference in May 2003, and there I discovered the National Study Group on Chronic Disorganization (NSGCD), now Institute for Challenging Disorganization (ICD), and Judith Kolberg. I picked up Judith's book *ADD-Friendly Ways* to *Organize Your Life,* and I could not put it down. I read the entire book on my flight home and realized I didn't have a clue about ADD or how to help my clients who have ADD. I knew I needed to join NSGCD and get educated!

Just a few months after joining NSGCD, I worked with a client, Angela, who was diagnosed with ADHD. You'll learn more my work with Angela in chapter 15.

If you have not already, join ICD and obtain at least their Level I certificates. If you discover you want to work with CD clients or clients with brain-based challenges, continue your education in those specific subjects and learn as much as you can to assist you in helping them with their organizing challenges.

During my first year in business, I discovered public speaking as a beneficial way to grow my contact base, meet potential clients, and create another revenue stream. What? Another revenue stream? I had not imagined multiple revenue streams when I started this profession. I thought I would work with people to organize their homes, and I did not have a vision for other directions that might lead to. Speaking was the second of many revenue streams I now have.

If you think public speaking is not for you because you are not comfortable speaking to an audience, my advice is to rethink that.

In my prior profession, I was the employee benefits manager for a high-tech company, and part of my responsibility was to present to the employees each year their benefits package. Typically, that meant the benefits costs for the employees were increasing, or their benefits coverage was being reduced. I was terrified to deliver that message every year to an audience of mostly men who could be quite intimidating with their questions and comments. So, when I was asked to speak to a MOPS (moms of preschoolers) group on organizing, I was quite hesitant. But here's what happened. I discovered that what I love as much as organizing—maybe more—is talking about organizing. When you're passionate about something, it's much easier to talk about it. Chapters 16, 17, and 18 are presentations you can deliver right now!

As I continued my NAPO board work, I moved into the role of director of membership. In that role, I noticed many members who joined one year did not renew their membership the next year. I was curious about why and contacted several to ask them why they didn't renew their membership. What I learned was that they were closing their businesses. There were two main reasons: 1) they could organize themselves, but they couldn't organize others because they didn't have a process, or they were very set in the way they wanted to organize; and 2) they didn't know how to manage their business.

I thought it was so unfortunate that this happened because many of them were truly passionate about their profession. Lightbulb moment! That's when it occurred to me that maybe I could teach others what they needed to know about starting a business, working with clients, and growing their business. The Institute for Professional Organizers was born! I spent the summer of 2004 writing the training curriculum and held my first training in August.

Now, this sounds much easier than it was because I was working with clients an average of twenty-four hours a week, and my children were on summer break from school. I was writing curriculum and developing the training marketing plan and materials evenings and weekends. My children were not very happy with me that summer!

While I was writing the training curriculum, I discovered there were two areas I, as a business owner and professional organizer, was lacking. First, I had not written a business plan and had no experience with writing one. I didn't think one was necessary until I needed to teach others how to start and manage a business. For me, it was an afterthought, and I think it is for many new small business owners. I didn't understand the value of a business plan.

I didn't write a business plan the first year and a half I was in business, and I didn't experience any growth in my business either. Since writing my business plan and updating it each year with measurable goals and objectives, my business has experienced significant growth every year. A business plan is your road map to success, and not having one is a roadmap to failure.

If you don't have a written business plan and you are not measuring business goals and objectives, start now! Learn how in chapter 3. You won't regret it!

The second area I was lacking was not having a teachable organizing process. This was challenging for me because organization is innate to me. I don't have to think about how to do it, as organizing comes naturally. I often think organizers who have not always been organized, and instead had to learn organizing skills, understand their clients' organizing struggles much more than I ever could—and that's a huge advantage.

First, I thought, *What is my definition of organizing?* Not *Webster*'s definition, mine. I define organizing as "a sequence of steps that create and sustain order." I had to physically do each part of how I organize and document it as I did it. What was developed from that process is my trademarked 5 Steps to Organizing. The process is my framework for working with clients, and you can learn it in chapter 12.

However, it's important to understand that one system does not fit all. It is essential to understand how your client's brain organizes and build systems that support their way of thinking. A system that works for one client may not work for another. For example, take file systems. One client's brain will want their filing system with the file tabs all in one row and manila file folders. Another client's brain will want the tabs staggered and the folders different colors. And a third client might want organized piles of paper, not files!!

Formulate your organizing process and communicate it to your clients at your first meeting. You don't have to give all the details—just the process steps. Clients don't know how organizing works, and it calms them and builds trust with you if they can visualize the beginning, middle, and end of the process.

I never imagined I would trademark anything! It wasn't easy to trademark a process, but with the aid of a trademark attorney, I was able to trademark the Institute for Professional Organizers' Master Professional Organizer designation and my 5 Steps to Organizing process. I wanted to trademark both to strengthen the credentials my training participants earn.

There was a tremendous amount of activity during my first two years of business!

I devoured ICD teleclasses because I was hungry to learn as much as I could due to my increased number of chronically disorganized clients with ADD. I took the CD exam at NAPO's 2006 conference. I was so nervous since it was the first exam I had taken in many years. I passed and earned the CD Specialist Level II Certificate! The more education I attained, the more my confidence grew to work with specialized client populations.

My training business was growing too, and by the end of 2006, twenty-eight participants had completed my program. In the beginning, the training was only available in person and only in Portland, Oregon, four times a year.

These were very intense years, as I was working up to forty hours a week with clients, running two businesses, and conducting training seminars. Plus, Alex and Hannah were fourteen and twelve years old!

This is when it would have been smart for me to start outsourcing some of my administrative tasks. My one regret with my business is that I have spent too much of my time on it and not enough time with my family and friends. My advice is to consider outsourcing one administrative task. See how that feels and works for you and your business. If it gives you more time to work on growing your business or more time for family and friends, then it will be worth it, and you may even consider outsourcing more tasks.

Late 2006, NAPO announced its Certified Professional Organizer designation and the requirements to earn it from the Board of Certification for Professional Organizers, known as BCPO. Learn about the requirements in chapter 1. I was excited to discover I had achieved the application requirements. However, another requirement is passing an exam of 125 questions with a score of 70 percent or better. The BCPO provided the examination outline and a list of books the test questions were derived from. I had less than six months to study and prepare for the inaugural exam in May at NAPO's conference. Again, I was nervous and excited to be a part of this significant industry event and to take another exam!

As a warm-up to the CPO exam, the day before, I took the ICD ADD Specialist Level II exam! A few weeks later, I was relieved and thrilled to learn I passed both.

During the same time I was studying for the CPO exam; I was also participating in the Coach Approach for Organizers™ training from Denslow Brown to expand my tools for working with clients. From this training program, I learned that the significance of coaching is to allow space for the client to discover what approach to organizing will work for them. Instead of telling the client what to do, ask powerful questions and listen to what the client is telling you works for them. Coaching speaks to our clients' openness for change by clarifying values, motivation, and what matters most. Coaching became my fourth stream of revenue.

My training program was in high demand, as there were very few programs that not only taught how to work with clients but also how to run a business. I frequently received calls from people asking if I would come to their location and provide my training program. I didn't see that as a realistic option because a key component of my training program was the client practicum. I didn't have clients outside of Oregon. I reflected on how I could train people outside of Oregon.

I asked Stefan what he knew about online training platforms, and he explained webinars to me. I think he regretted it because he realized it was going to mean a lot of work not only for me but for him as my webmaster. He was right; it was a lot of work converting my training curriculum into an online format. But we did it!

I held live webinars every month. After a year, I got smarter and recorded my presentations. This opened up on-demand webinars, so anyone anywhere could learn anytime! Online training became my fifth stream of revenue, and the business and client forms from the training curriculum were also made available for purchase online separately, resulting in my sixth stream of revenue. This revenue is one way to make money while you sleep, and it's known as passive income.

From 2009 to 2011 professional organizers in the United States were in make-or-break years. In 2008 and 2009, the United States labor market lost 8.4 million jobs. People were cutting out all discretionary expenses, and that included professional organizing services.

My phone was not ringing, and people were not signing up for my webinars, online training, or live seminars. Many professional organizers left the industry because they were experiencing the same and needed to find employment to pay their bills. Or, if they did not provide the primary source of income for their family and that person lost his or her job, they now needed to find a way to have a steady income.

Interestingly though, many people who lost their jobs and couldn't find employment wanted to start their own business. They had time on their hands and were watching HGTV and, you guessed it, *Mission Organization*, *Clean Sweep with Peter Walsh*, and *Neat*. These shows sparked a desire in many to start a professional organizing business, but they had little financial resources to do so and didn't know how to start a business. The calls I received from people about my training program were to say they would love to take my training program, but they just could not afford it.

I, too, suddenly had time on my hands, and I was fortunate that Stefan's employment was not impacted by the recession. As Stefan can attest to, when I have time on my hands, I find a way to fill it! I decided that if the participants couldn't come to me and couldn't afford the online version of my training program, there must be a way to get the information to them. Because what I'm passionate about is making sure those in this profession represent the industry as experienced and knowledgeable professionals.

I decided to write a book that covered my training program content, not the depth of the content but the surface—enough to give the information needed to get started. Writing a book was not an easy task. In fact, it was painful. I was accustomed to writing in bullet points and then speaking at some length to each bullet point. But I persevered, and with the help of an editor, *Get Rich Organizing* was self-published in August 2009. It is now this book updated, resulting in my seventh stream of revenue.

I didn't write the book to get rich. In fact, I knew I wouldn't sell millions of copies because millions of people don't want to become professional organizers—thank goodness! I wrote the book to fill a need for a niche population. I'm glad I did! I have met and heard from hundreds of people who have purchased *Get Rich Organizing*, about how it was an invaluable resource to them in the development of their business and how they would not have succeeded without that information. Those words are worth all the pain it took to write the book!

In 2010, Power Dynamics Publishing Company contacted me, asking if I would want to coauthor the book *Get Organized TODAY*. Eighteen other professional organizers and I each wrote a chapter of the book. My chapter is "Win at Organizing, Overcoming Chronic Disorganization."

Never in my wildest dreams did I dream of being a published author, because I didn't think I had the skills to write a book. My advice is to hire experts and never think you can't do something because you don't know how to, or you don't think you have the skills to. Isn't that what we teach our clients after all?

With multiple revenue streams, my business has not experienced a loss, even during the economic downturn of 2007–2009.

The recession may have ended in 2009, but the US economy was still in recovery well into 2011. People were quite hesitant to spend their discretionary income on organizing services. I did have clients stay with me who financially could during the recession, and some are still my clients today; they are chronically disorganized, and, for some, they always will be.

I needed to attract clients and rebuild my client base. For the first time, I decided to discount my fee by packaging my services. And it worked! I made more money on organizing services than ever before. Psychologically, people like to think they are getting a deal, especially when they feel they don't have money to spend. I required prepayment of the full package price before I started working with them. Prepayment provided cash flow for my business, and it did something even better: it committed the client to the work. Clients canceling their sessions at the last minute are a thing of the past because of prepayment.

If you want to avoid last-minute cancellations, require all or partial payment before your client session.

I added the Master Professional Organizer® layer to my training program in 2012 as a way for participants to attain an industry credential before they might be able to attain the Certified Professional Organizer credential and to further stand out from their competition. To become a Master Professional Organizer, a person needs to successfully complete Layers 1 and 2 of my training program, demonstrating they have mastered my 5 Steps to Organizing process, can plan and lead an organizing project, and are able to communicate and transfer organizing skills to a client.

In 2013, something startling and unexpected happened. I woke up one day and was not excited to go work with my client. What happened? I love to organize. That was not what I wasn't excited about. It was the client. I found myself thinking of this client all the time. How could I help her? Why wasn't she doing the homework between our sessions? How could I get her husband to understand how ADD affected her ability to organize and to not abuse her emotionally by saying she was lazy and stupid?

I started thinking I might want to stop working with clients, and that made me sad. I was at the NAPO conference, and a presenter started talking about compassion fatigue. She went on to explain that compassion fatigue comes on due to ongoing exposure to client struggles. Compassion fatigue is a specialized form of burnout in which the professional organizer no longer feels able to help his or her clients. That hopeless feeling might not be conscious but instead might manifest as cynicism or a growing disdain for clients, or it could be that you experience impatience, an inability to empathize with clients, or overall job dissatisfaction. That was mostly what I was experiencing.

I decided that, for my well-being, I needed to end this client relationship and set clear boundaries with myself about who I would take on as a client in the future. It also occurred to me that there are some clients and projects that are not for me, but they are for others. I did not want to hire employees, but I did want to work with others on projects or have others work on projects that were not appealing to me—like garages!

I reached out to a few women who completed my training program and asked if they would be interested in working as a subcontractor for me. This was one of the best business decisions I have ever made.

I chose the business model of subcontractors instead of employees to keep overhead costs lower and because I couldn't guarantee specific work hours.

My team and I can complete large projects in a fraction of the time it would take me to complete on my own with a client, if a project doesn't appeal to me, I assign it to a subcontractor, and the subcontractor gets work they otherwise would not. It's a win-win-win! It's also another revenue stream because the subcontractor's fee is shared with my company. My advice is, if you're waking up in the morning and not jumping up and down, excited to organize with a client, you might want to stop and think about what's going on. Maybe you're starting to experience compassion fatigue. If you experience the symptoms, a consultation with a trusted peer or mentor can help, and professional counseling should be among the options you consider if you're not able to get back on track on your own.

I also advise working with clients who make your heart sing and working on organizing projects you enjoy; you don't have to work with everyone who contacts you. Consider working with other organizers as well, especially on large projects, because together we are better!

After more than ten years, my businesses were running like well-oiled machines, and with ten different streams of revenue resulting in increased profits year after year, I felt it was time I could return to volunteering in the professional organizer industry. But where and how?

One day an email from ICD came into my inbox, communicating they were looking for nominations for treasurer for ICD's board of directors. Hmm, I thought, *I have held every board position but treasurer. Could I do the job? Would ICD want me?*

Valentina Sgro was president of ICD at the time. I knew Valentina, so I decided to give her a call and inquire about the treasurer's role. After talking with Valentina, I submitted my nomination. Next, the nominating committee contacted me and arranged for a series of in-depth interviews, after which I was notified they would be delighted to submit my nomination to the ICD board. At the next board meeting I was elected, along with the other new board members.

It was a bit challenging at first because treasurer work was new to me, but I love working with numbers and financials and discovered I have an aptitude for the role. I enjoyed the work, the other people on the board, and the management company staff. It felt good to be of service to the industry while connecting with other industry professionals and developing my leadership skills.

Sheila Delson, former ICD president, launched her Virtual Organizing training program in 2014, which resulted in my eleventh stream of revenue.

As a veteran organizer with many years of working hands-on with clients, it was becoming increasingly more difficult to keep up with client demand and physical aspects associated with hands-on work. Additionally, not all clients can afford ongoing hands-on work. Virtual Organizing was the solution to all three! Plus, I can now provide organizing services to anyone, anywhere. The first week after completing my training with Sheila, I had several new clients locally and afar who engaged my new virtual organizing services.

When I was attending the 2014 ICD conference, I received an email from the Association of Professional Declutters' (APDO's) conference chair inviting me to be the keynote speaker at their 2015 conference—keynote speaker, London, England! What a thrill and honor to be asked. We arranged for a Skype meeting, discussed what they wanted me to speak about, and I accepted.

Being an international keynote speaker was an invaluable experience, and my ICD board involvement led me to that opportunity. Later, in 2017, I was invited to deliver the keynote at the Japanese Association of Life Organizers' (JALO's) conference in Sendai, Japan. I formed lifelong friendships and connections at APDO and JALO conferences. Both opportunities were tremendous honors. I love learning from my colleagues around the globe!

The Container Store is an organizing products store. I equate it to a professional organizer's candy store. They have stores all over the United States. Late in 2015, I was contacted by the Container Store, asking if I would be interested in interviewing for their Contained Home Consultant position. I was hesitant because I felt I would be working for my competition. I also didn't think it would be possible to earn the same or close to my hourly rate as a subcontractor with the Container Store. I was wrong; I could. I could also receive commissions on products and closet systems I sold.

I interviewed for the position and was asked why I wanted the position when I had a very successful business. I told them I thought the customers would want primarily closet-designing services and not strenuous hands-on organizing. That appealed to me since it was increasingly more difficult to do the physical work as I aged. Secondly, I believed there was a customer population that would prefer to hire a professional organizer associated with a large store chain and corporation. I believed they felt safer having someone from the Container Store in their home than a stranger.

The Container Store offered me the contractor position, I accepted, and I have been with them for over two years. My organizing services revenue has doubled as a result, and it's been primarily from closet designing and product sales, just as I suspected.

Keep in mind that what appears as competition might actually be collaboration.

In 2003, when I started working as a professional organizer, my clients were moms with young children, much like myself. I helped them set up household systems and routines and organize their physical space. At that time, I knew I didn't want to work with seniors because I didn't think I could relate to where they were in life and how to help them.

As my business grew, my clients were shifting to solopreneurs, much like myself. I helped them get their business operations and workspaces organized.

Later, as my children left and went to college and I became an empty nester, those were the clients I attracted. I helped them right-size their home now that their children had moved out. I also helped them with those organizing projects they had put off doing "until they had time," such as organizing photographs and other memorabilia.

Well, now that I am in my senior years, I understand where seniors are in their lives, and I want to learn more about how to help them either age in place or with moving and transitioning to a senior community.

In 2017, I joined the National Association of Senior Move Managers (NASMM) for education and to strengthen my skills in working with the senior population.

Recognize that as you mature and age, your ideal client might mature and age too.

Sixteen years after I started my organizing business, my children have grown and launched into their adult lives, and Stefan and I are celebrating twenty-one years together.

In the beginning, I was far from mastering the business of organizing. I have learned and grown from my experiences, and with my business comprising fourteen distinct streams of revenue, I feel I have mastered the business of organizing. That's not to say there isn't anything left for me to learn; there is always more to learn!

I hope by sharing my journey and my knowledge in the following chapters, you will avoid the growing pains I experienced.

INTRODUCTION

Mastering the Business of Organizing will:

- provide you with the knowledge you need to become a successful professional organizing business owner
- help you cut out months or even years of annoying mistakes and learning curves, because you need to make money immediately
- show you how to position yourself to attract your ideal client with over one hundred marketing ideas
- introduce you to social media and website development
- instruct you on how to clearly communicate your value and how to charge for your valuable services
- teach you new organizing skills and techniques to work with a variety of client types
- provide you with legal, insurance, and tax information to get you started in the right business entity for you and to give you an understanding of the protection your business needs
- teach you proven processes and systems to organize others and transfer organizing skills
- tell you about real client stories that will inspire you to teach others organizing skills and keep you from making some serious mistakes in dealing with clients
- move you to action with recommended exercises and actions found at the end of the chapters

Additionally, you receive:

- forms available for you to personalize with your company information, saving you hours of time of creating on your own
- a listing of my top twenty-five organizing products and where to find them so you don't have to spend time researching

- material to create workshops on paper, time, and clutter so you can immediately market and demonstrate your organizing knowledge
- industry associations and information

The forms within this book are available for you to personalize with your company information. Any forms that are of contractual nature should be reviewed by your attorney to ensure they meet with your company practices and are defensible by your attorney where you conduct business.

I wrote *Mastering the Business of Organizing* along with the Institute for Professional Organizers™ curriculum, training manuals, and program because I believe in the immense value of this profession. I want others who aspire to it to represent the industry as experienced and knowledgeable professionals. I also want to share my learning in the hopes that others will benefit greatly from my experiences. I wish I had this book when I started my professional organizing business, SolutionsForYou, Inc.; I would have saved time, money, and a lot of hard work. It has everything a professional organizer needs to plan, launch, manage, grow, and leverage a profitable business.

To deepen your knowledge of this subject and to gain hands-on client experience, consider attending one of my seminars. Program information is available at www.instituteprofessionalorganizers.com.

I wish you tremendous success in your career as a professional organizing business owner!

PART I

The Business of Organizing

CHAPTER 1

Introduction to Professional Organizing

Description: This chapter will define the profession of organizing, provide an overview of the history of the organizing industry and of the National Association of Productivity & Organizing Professionals (NAPO), identify the characteristics of a professional organizer and of a business owner, and review the requirements for industry certification.

- professional organizer definition
- getting started in the professional organizing business
- characteristics
    - professional organizer characteristics
    - business owner characteristics
- top ten considerations in becoming a professional organizer
- NAPO history and overview
- NAPO membership
    - chapter membership
- professional organizer specialties
- NAPO code of ethics
- certification
- additional industry associations

Professional Organizer Definition

According to the National Association of Productivity & Organizing Professionals (NAPO),

- "A Professional Organizer supports evaluation, decision-making, and action around objects, space, and data; helping clients achieve desired outcomes regarding function, order, and clarity.
- A Productivity Consultant supports evaluation, decision-making, and action around time, energy, and resources; helping clients achieve desired outcomes regarding goals, effectiveness, and priorities."[1]

A professional organizer's services can range from designing an efficient closet to organizing a cross-country move. For homeowners, he or she might offer room-by-room space planning and reorganization, estate organization, improved management of paperwork and computer files, systems for managing personal finances and other records, or coaching in time management and goal setting.

In business settings, a productivity consultant can increase productivity and profitability with improvements in paper filing and storage, electronic organizing, work-flow systems, employee time management, space design, and more.

Some professional organizers work with specific populations, such as those with attention deficit disorder (ADD), the chronically disorganized, children, seniors, or students.

Getting Started in the Professional Organizing Business

There are many ways to enter the field of professional organizing. Many operate their own businesses, while others act as independent contractors or are employed by an organizing company. Those who run their own companies require business skills in addition to organizing skills. For many professional organizers, running a business is the most challenging part of the job; it is important for you to weigh this decision carefully. A small business owner wears many hats, as they often serve as marketer, accountant, bookkeeper, and more.

The good news is that opportunity abounds in this industry, and you can make the choice that is comfortable for you. Should you choose to operate your own business, there are courses such as the Institute for Professional Organizers geared toward helping you succeed.

Those considering a future as a professional organizer must take stock of their financial needs. Start-ups often spend 80 percent of the first year's income on marketing. Generally, the first year runs at a loss, as it takes six to nine months to start generating an active client base. It is helpful to have financial resources such as credit lines and

---

[1] "About NAPO," National Association of Productivity & Organizing Professionals, accessed June 12, 2018, https://www.napo.net/page/about_aboutnapo.

savings to draw from as you get started, and if you are currently employed, you might want to consider continuing in that job until you have an established business.

Characteristics

This first list is of the most common characteristics a successful professional organizer demonstrates. The second list is of common characteristics a successful business owner demonstrates. Which ones do you possess? Which ones do you need to strengthen?

Professional Organizer Characteristics

- *Confident.* Always remember you know more than the client—but don't flaunt it. That will help increase your confidence, and you will appear more confident.
- *Courteous.* The ability to be gracious even when your client may not be.
- *Creative.* The ability to visualize spatially and the ability to think how to repurpose something that could become an organizing tool/container are important.
- *Credible.* Belonging to an association of your profession and obtaining education and training/certification gains you credibility.
- *Diplomatic.* You often need to be diplomatic when working with two or more clients at the same time, and sometimes you feel like a mediator.
- *Efficient.* If you are being paid by the hour, your client needs to see that you are efficient with your time / their money.
- *Empathetic.* Communicate to the client that they are not alone and that many others are in a similar state. Let them know that it's okay to ask for help.
- *Encouraging.* The ability to ask the right questions and encourage the client to come up with their own answer is important.
- *Ethical.* Maintain complete confidentiality (see NAPO's Code of Ethics later in this chapter).
- *Fun.* Organizing should be fun and not drudgery.
- *Good listener.* The ability to listen to and infer what a client means.
- *Good planner.* The ability to see the big picture and break goals down into manageable steps is needed, as is the ability to categorize and plan ahead.
- *Honest.* Your client needs to hear the truth from you.
- *Know your limitations.* Don't do anything physically outside of your limits or anything you are not trained or skilled to do.
- *Nonjudgmental.* The key to earning your client's trust is demonstrating that you are nonjudgmental of their situation.
- *Objective.* Listen to your client's view and needs with an open mind.

- *On time and prepared.* This goes hand in hand with professionalism. Walk your talk.
- *Open-minded.* Customize organizational systems to meet client needs, not yours.
- *Patient.* Being patient is very helpful when working with clients who have difficulty making decisions, have ADD, and with seniors.
- *Positive attitude.* Your client needs to hear from you that it is possible to get organized.
- *Professional.* This is how the world sees you and your business; you represent not only you but the entire industry.
- *Respectful.* Always ask before acting. This includes taking pictures, opening drawers and cabinets, and touching anything.

Business Owner Characteristics

- *Creative.* The ability to think outside the box. How can you stand out from all of the other professional organizers?
- *Delegates.* Let others do what you are not best at (bookkeeping, web design, marketing, legal documents, etc.).
- *Dreamer.* See the big picture.
- *Efficient.* Be efficient with your client's time but also yours in your office.
- *Good planner.* Plan ahead with your business. What are your goals and objectives?
- *Know your limitations.* This goes hand in hand with delegating.
- *Manages time well.* Plan your day for your highest efficiency.
- *Organized.* Be prepared for working with each client, get things done on time, and be able to find what you need when you need it.
- *Problem solver.* Running a business has its risks; if you can identify what they are and have a plan to solve them, they will no longer be risks.
- *Resourceful.* Who do you need to help you do your job (handyperson, painter, interior designer, etc.)? What products do you need? What are they? Where can you find them?
- *Self-disciplined.* You are your own boss now. This means you need to be disciplined to get yourself to the office every day to generate business.
- *Self-motivated.* If you can't motivate yourself, who do you know who can be your cheerleaders?
- *Self-starter.* If procrastination is an issue for you, you need to learn how to get started on areas that you are not comfortable with.

Top Ten Considerations in Becoming a Professional Organizer[2]

1. There are many ways to enter the field of professional organizing. The majority of NAPO members run their own businesses, while others act as independent contractors or are employed by an organizing company. If you choose to run your own company, you will use your organizing skills and also need to draw on business skills. The running of a business is perhaps the most important and, for some, the most daunting. There is more to running a business than being organized.
2. Be prepared to wear many hats as a small-business owner, such as accountant, marketer, bookkeeper, and the like. Don't be afraid to outsource these jobs; it pays to hire someone to do what you can't.
3. Do you prefer to work alone or with others? Many organizers thrive when working in teams. Consider collaborating with another person when you set up shop.
4. Take stock of your financial needs. Start-ups often spend 80 percent of the first year's income on marketing, with the expectation that those percentages will reverse themselves. In order to know whether this career will meet your financial goals, determine what you must make (net) in a year and work backward from that. For example, if you need to bring home $26,000/year, you need to have $500/week coming in after all expenses and taxes are paid. That figure does not factor in vacation time, sick days, and cancellations.
5. It is helpful to have financial resources such as credit lines and savings to draw from as a start-up business. Consider obtaining a line of credit before you need it; it's easier to qualify when you don't need it than when you do.
6. These are some of the most common abilities and qualities that successful professional organizers demonstrate. Do you have what it takes?

   - ability to listen and infer what a client means
   - ability to customize organizational systems to meet client needs, not yours
   - consulting/coaching skills—ability to ask the right questions to encourage the client to come up with the answer
   - ability to teach and pass on skills
   - ability to visualize spatially
   - ability to see the big picture and break goals down into manageable steps
   - ability to categorize and plan ahead

---

[2] "About NAPO," National Association of Productivity & Organizing Professionals, accessed June 12, 2018, https://www.napo.net/page/about_aboutnapo.

- physical and mental endurance
- compassion
- responsibility
- professionalism

7. A professional image will be important, because this is how the world sees you and your business. Credibility and professionalism go hand in hand. You'll want to put the "professional" in professional organizer. You represent not only yourself but also the entire industry.
8. Start with the area of organizing that you are passionate about but keep an open mind to other niches to expand your horizons.
9. Expand your skills as your business develops, through reading, teleclasses, conferences, networking, and NAPO involvement.
10. Joining NAPO will keep you abreast of new products, books, and business trends in the organizing industry.

NAPO History and Overview[3]

"The National Association of Productivity & Organizing Professionals (NAPO) was established in 1985 and is a nonprofit educational association whose members include organizing consultants, speakers, trainers, authors, and manufacturers of organizing products. As of this writing, NAPO has about 3,500 members across the United States and in various foreign countries. It is one of the largest international association of and for organizers. NAPO's mission is to be the leading source for organizing and productivity professionals by providing exceptional education, enhancing business connections, advancing industry research, and raising public awareness."

National Membership

You can join NAPO at www.napo.net. NAPO offers several types of memberships. Most new members join as provisional members and enjoy basic member benefits while gaining professional development via NAPO University's Professional Practices Coursework. Once this coursework has been completed, members advance to professional member status and enjoy full member benefits, including a listing in the Professional Organizer and Productivity Consultant Search Tool.

---

[3] "About NAPO," National Association of Productivity & Organizing Professionals, accessed June 12, 2018, https://www.napo.net/page/about_aboutnapo.

Chapter Membership

As of this writing, NAPO has thirty-two chapters including a virtual chapter. Chapter membership is voluntary, and national membership is required for chapter membership. Some chapter meetings and programs are available to nonmembers. To find a NAPO chapter in your area, visit www.napo.net.

Professional Organizer Specialties

As a professional organizer, you might specialize in one or several of the following areas of organizing specialty:

- closet designing
- closet organizing
- collections/memorabilia/photos
- computer consulting/training
- corporations
- ergonomics
- errands/personal shopping
- estate organization
- estate sales
- event/meeting planning
- filing systems
- finances/bookkeeping
- garages/attics/basements
- garage/tag sales
- health insurance claims (preparation assistance)
- home offices
- information management
- kitchen organizing
- legal offices / medical offices
- moving/relocations
- offices
- residential seminars / public speaking
- space designing
- space organizing
- time management / goal setting
- wardrobe consulting

- work with children
- work with people who have ADD
- work with seniors
- work with students

NAPO Code of Ethics[4]

The NAPO Code of Ethics is a set of principles that guides our professional conduct with our clients and colleagues. Members of NAPO pledge to exercise judgment, self-restraint, and conscience in their conduct in order to establish and maintain public confidence in the integrity of NAPO members and to preserve and encourage fair and equitable practices among all who are engaged in our profession.

Clients
Working Relationships

- I will serve my clients with integrity, competence, and objectivity, and will treat them with respect and courtesy.
- I will offer services in those areas in which I am qualified and will accurately represent those qualifications in both verbal and written communications.
- When unable or unqualified to fulfill requests for services, I will make every effort to recommend the services of other qualified professional organizers, productivity consultants and/or other qualified professionals.
- I will advertise my services in an honest manner and will represent the organizing and productivity profession accurately.

Confidentiality

- I will keep confidential all client information, both business and personal, including that which may be revealed by other professional organizers and productivity consultants.
- I will use proprietary client information only with the client's permission.
- I will keep client information confidential and not use it to benefit myself or my firm or reveal this information to others.

---

[4] "NAPO Code of Ethics," National Association of Productivity & Organizing Professionals, accessed June 12, 2018, https://www.napo.net/page/about_ethics?&hhsearchterms=%22code+and+ethics%22.

Fees

- I will decide independently and communicate to my client in advance my fees and expenses and will charge fees and expenses which I deem reasonable, legitimate, and commensurate with my experience, the services I deliver, and the responsibility I accept.
- I will make recommendations for products and services with my client's best interests in mind.

Colleagues

- I will seek and maintain an equitable, honorable, and cooperative association with other NAPO members and will treat them with respect and courtesy.
- I will respect the intellectual property rights (materials, titles, and thematic creations) of my colleagues, and other firms and individuals, and will not use proprietary information or methodologies without permission.
- I will act and speak on a high professional level so as not to bring discredit to the organizing and productivity profession.

Certification

The professional organizing industry has a certification program that was developed by NAPO and is operated under the auspices of the Board of Certification for Professional Organizers (BCPO). The Certified Professional Organizer (CPO) designation is a voluntary, industry-led effort that benefits the public and members of the organizing profession. CPO certification recognizes those professionals who have met specific minimum qualifications and have proven through examination and client interaction that they possess the body of knowledge and experience required for certification. The program recognizes and raises industry standards, practices, and ethics. While the CPO designation is not an endorsement or recommendation, certification of professional organizers maximizes the value received from the services provided and products recommended by a CPO.

For more information, download The BCPO Handbook for the Certification Program at http://c.ymcdn.com/sites/www.napo.net/resource/resmgr/NAPO-17-BCPOhandbook.pdf.

Additional Industry Associations

(alphabetical order)

1. Association of Professional Declutters & Organisers UK (APDO) www.apdo-uk.co.uk
2. Associação Nacional de Profissionais de Organização e Produtividade from Brazil http://www.anpop.com.br
3. Board of Certification for Professional Organizers (BCPO) www.certifiedprofessionalorganizers.org
4. Children and Adults with Attention-Deficit/Hyperactivity Disorder (CHADD) http://www.chadd.org/
5. Institute for Challenging Disorganization (ICD) www.challengingdisorganization.com
6. Japanese Association of Life Organizers (JALO) http://jalo.jp
7. Korean Association of Professional Organizers http://www.kapo100.org/
8. National Association of Productivity & Organizing Professionals (NAPO) www.napo.net
9. National Association of Senior Move Managers (NASMM) www.nasmm.org
10. National Attention Deficit Disorder Association (ADDA) www.add.org
11. Nederlandse Beroepsvereniging van Professional Organizers The Netherlands (NBPO) (Dutch Professional Organizers of The Netherlands) https://www.nbpo.nl/
12. Professional Organizers in Canada (POC) www.organizersincanada.com

 EXERCISES

> ↳ From the list of characteristics, which ones could you improve upon?
>
> ↳ What area(s) will you specialize in?

📄 **ACTIONS**

> - ☐ Join NAPO or other industry association(s).
> - ☐ Research liability insurance.
> - ☐ Set up a tracking system for certification hours and supporting documentation.
> - ☐ Read from the BCPO recommended reading list, even if you are not planning to certify at this time.

CHAPTER 2

Assessing Your Skills

Description: This chapter will review your skills, prior experience, and education as it relates to the field of professional organizer, and it will discuss why you want to be one.

- How can your background and education work for you?
- Why do you want to be a professional organizer?
- What professional organizer characteristics do you possess?
- What business owner characteristics do you possess?
- What is a typical day like for a professional organizer?
- What is a typical day like for a business owner?
- What types of education and training are available?

Most professional organizers who fail do so not because they can't organize but because they don't know how to start and run a business. Understanding your strengths, background, experience, and characteristics will help you to succeed not only as a professional organizer but as a professional organizing business owner.

What Are Your Strengths?

- What characteristics from chapter 1 do you possess?
- Do you meet people easily the first time? If not, why? You might want to only work with referrals from people you know.
- What people skills do you possess (courteous, friendly, good listener, diplomatic, empathetic, encouraging, honest, nonjudgmental, patient, respectful)?
- Are you comfortable speaking in front of a group? Public speaking is a great marketing venue if you are.

- Have you managed projects before? What were they? What project management skills do you possess (manage time well, ability to break down a large project into tasks, delegate, efficient, problem solver, resourceful)?
- Have you always been an organized person, or have you learned how to be one? If you have not always been an organized person, you will be able to relate better to your clients than professional organizers who have always been organized.

What Is Your Background?

Consider how the following experiences and personal transitions might influence how you can help others to develop organizing systems:

- Where have you lived?
- Have you moved often?
- Are you married, single, or divorced?
- Do you have children?
- Did you attend/graduate from college?

These are life transitions, and life transitions are a key factor in why and when organization systems break down for your clients.

What Is Your Job Experience?

- Have you always worked outside the home—or never?
- Have you been a stay-at-home parent or a working parent?
- Have you worked in corporate, and did you like it? If you have not worked in corporate, you may not be comfortable working with corporate clients.
- Have you worked in small businesses, or have you owned your own business?
- Do you like being the boss?
- Do you work well with others or prefer to work alone?

A Typical Day for a Professional Organizer

A typical day working with clients might include any one or more of the following activities:

- cleaning out closets, kitchens, storage areas, bedrooms, attics, and garages—in other words, basic decluttering

- remodeling closets and storage spaces
- rearranging living space to be more pleasing and efficient
- personal coaching and goal setting
- planning, packing, and unpacking for relocation
- garage and estate sales
- errands and personal shopping
- computer organizing and training
- setting up filing systems and developing paper-flow systems
- information management systems
- accounting and bookkeeping
- filing
- setting up record-keeping systems
- sorting through paper piles
- paying bills
- developing procedures manuals
- preparing medical insurance forms
- event planning
- disaster preparedness
- photo and memorabilia organization
- time-management training
- seminars and public speaking
- task management and tracking

In addition, organizers may work with:

- people in their homes
- small businesses
- large businesses
- clients with attention deficit disorder
- people who are chronically disorganized
- students
- seniors
- individuals
- groups

Professional organizers don't organize all of these spaces and work with all of the groups of people and businesses. Most will specialize in one or more areas.

A Typical Day for a Business Owner

Business owners will typically need to address one or more of the following areas on any given day:

- invoicing clients
- recording expenses and income
- balancing your checking account
- reviewing your financials
- writing marketing materials
- writing a newsletter
- preparing for tax filing or meeting with your tax accountant
- running payroll (even if you are a one-person organization)
- interviewing and hiring employees or subcontractors
- scheduling employees or subcontractors
- developing your website and updating regularly
- reviewing and updating your business plan and goals

Your background, experience, skills, characteristics, and business goals will determine what your typical day will be like as a professional organizing business owner and determine where you need to gain skills and resources to be successful as both.

Training and Education

If after assessing your skills, you discover you need additional training and education on how to work with clients and run a business, there are resources available.

Working with Clients Training and Education

- The Institute for Professional Organizers (IPO) www.instituteprofessionalorganizers.com
    Each layer of IPO's Fast Track Method training and education program develops your skills and confidence to work with clients and Master the Business of Organizing. Layer by layer, they provide you with increased protection that your business will thrive. You will not find another professional organizer training program with their unique layered approach, comprehensiveness, and affordability.

- Institute for Challenging Disorganization (ICD)
    www.challengingdisorganization.com
    ICD's mission is to provide education, research, and strategies to benefit people with chronic disorganization.
- Coach Approach for Organizers Training with Denslow Brown
    http://www.coachapproachfororganizers.com/
- Virtual Organizing Training with Sheila Delson
    http://freedomainconcepts.com/virtual-organizing-training/

Small Business Training and Education

- The Institute for Professional Organizers (IPO) www.instituteprofessionalorganizers.com
    Each layer of IPO's Fast Track Method training and education program develops your skills and confidence to work with clients and Master the Business of Organizing. Layer by layer, they provide you with increased protection that your business will thrive. You will not find another professional organizer training program with their unique layered approach, comprehensiveness, and affordability.
- US Small Business Administration
    https://www.sba.gov/about-sba
    The US Small Business Administration has delivered millions of loans, loan guarantees, contracts, counseling sessions, and other forms of assistance to small businesses.
- SCORE
    https://www.sba.gov/tools/local-assistance/score
    SCORE members are trained to serve as counselors, advisors, and mentors to aspiring entrepreneurs and business owners.
- Mercy Corps
    https://www.mercycorpsnw.org/business/training/business-classes/
    Mercy Corps Northwest provides classes, seminars, and consulting by industry experts that will help you improve your skills and give you the support you need to successfully start and grow your small business. Training programs are generously supported by a Women's Business Center grant from the US Small Business Administration.

 EXERCISES

- What does all of this say about you? Take a few minutes and write on a piece of paper what you have done in your life that will make you a good professional organizer. What are your unique abilities?

- What do you like to do from the list of typical activities for a professional organizer and a business owner?

- What don't you like to do from the list of typical activities for a professional organizer and a business owner?

- What additional training and education do you need to work with clients or run your business?

CHAPTER 3

Writing a Business Plan

Description: Your business plan is often an afterthought if it is ever addressed at all. In this chapter, you will learn the value of writing a business plan and how it can save you from costly mistakes.

- Define your business concept.
- Develop your mission statement.
- Determine who your key client is and how you will attract them.
- Describe what services and products you will offer.
- Research your competition.
- Define your goals and objectives.
- Develop your financial plan.
- Detail your action plan.
- Identify your resource requirements.
- Perform a SWOT analysis.

The real value of creating a business plan is not in having the finished written plan in hand. Rather, the value lies in the process of researching and thinking about your business in a systematic way. The act of planning helps you think things through thoroughly, study and research if you are not sure of the facts, and look at your ideas critically. It takes time now but avoids costly, perhaps disastrous, mistakes later.

I didn't write a business plan the first two years I was in business, and I didn't experience any growth in my business either. Since writing my business plan and updating it each year, my business has experienced significant growth each and every year.

It typically takes several weeks to complete a good plan. Most of that time is spent in research and rethinking your ideas and assumptions. But then that's the value of the process. Make time to do the job properly. Those who do never regret the effort. And finally, be sure to keep detailed notes on your sources of information and on the assumptions underlying your financial data and review with your attorney and accountant.

Questions to Ask Before Writing Your Business Plan

- Is this a hobby, a job, a business, or are you an entrepreneur?
- What does it take to manage each of these entities?
- What are the time commitments for each of these, whether you are a doer, manager, president, or all three? How can you schedule time for each of these roles?

Business Concept

- Summarize the key technology, concept, or strategy on which your business is based. This can be as basic as people need help organizing their paper, time, and space, or, people need to learn organizing skills.

Mission Statement

Your mission statement is a clear statement of your company's long-term mission. Many companies have a brief mission statement, usually in fifty words or less, explaining their reason for being and their guiding principles.

Example:
To provide confidential and empathetic advice to our clients, identify their individual organizing challenges, and attain and maintain organization by working with them to create solutions and sustainable systems that will increase their productivity, reduce stress, and lead to more control over their surroundings.

It says *what you will do for the client* (provide confidential and empathetic advice to our clients, identify their individual organizing challenges, and attain and maintain organization) and *how* (by working with them to create solutions and sustainable systems), and *the benefits* of working with you (will increase their productivity, reduce stress, and lead to more control over their surroundings).

Market and Customer Analysis

Review those changes in market share, leadership, players, market shifts, costs, pricing, or competition that provide the opportunity for your company's success. Identify your key clients, their characteristics, and their geographic locations, otherwise known as their demographics. You may have more than one client group (residential, home-based business, small business, corporate). Identify the most important groups. Then, for each client group, construct what is called a demographic profile.

For residential customers, the demographic factors might be:

- age
- gender
- location
- income level
- social class and occupation
- education
- learning disability

For business customers, the demographic factors might be:

- industry (or portion of an industry)
- location
- size of firm
- quality, technology, and price preferences

Strategy

Outline a marketing strategy that is consistent with your niche. Will you have important indirect competitors? For example, on-demand movies compete with theaters, although they are different types of businesses. How will your products or services compare with the competition? See chapter 9 for more information on marketing strategies.

Opportunities (Problems and Opportunities)

State your client's problems and define the nature of product and service opportunities that are created by those problems. What are the needs and how can you fill them? What are some problems and symptoms that your clients have? What do they want from you? What is so important that they are willing to pay you to provide solutions for them? These are people you need to be marketing to. You don't have to work with everyone!

Example

A common consumer problem is clients have tried to set up a file system, but they never use it.

The opportunity for you is to offer your clients a universal prepackaged filing system that (a) solves the client's problem and (b) can provide you with product revenue because you can buy the filing systems in quantity and receive a wholesale price from the vendor and keep the mark-up for your business.

Products and Services

Describe your products and services as you see them and, more importantly, how your client sees them. What factors will give you competitive advantages or disadvantages? Examples may include level of quality or unique or proprietary features. What are the fees of your products or services? Describe the most important features. What is special about your services? Describe the benefits. That is, what will your services do for the client? What after-sale services will you give? Some examples are guarantee, support, follow-up, maintenance, and a refund policy.

Competition

Summarize your competition. What are they doing? How can you do it better? Outline your company's competitive advantage. List your major competitors. Will they compete with you across the board, or just for certain products, certain clients, or in certain locations? Will you have important indirect competitors? How will your products or services compare with the competition?

Niche

Now that you have systematically analyzed your industry, your clients, and the competition, you should have a clear picture of where your company fits into the world. In one short paragraph, define your niche, your unique corner of the market.

Goals and Objectives

Goals are destinations. Where do you want your business to be? Objectives are progress markers along the way to achieving your goals. For example, a goal might be to move from working part-time to full-time after two years. An objective of that goal might be to increase client billable time from ten hours a week to twenty hours a week.

Financial Plan

The financial plan consists of your start-up costs, a twelve-month profit and loss projection, a cash-flow projection, a projected balance sheet, and a break-even calculation. Together they constitute a reasonable estimate of your company's financial future. More important, the process of thinking through the financial plan will improve your insight into the inner financial workings of your company. QuickBooks and Quicken for Small Businesses are excellent software programs for tracking revenue and expenses and for producing business and tax reports.

The following table includes *expenses* professional organizers should consider in their business financial planning for their business *start-up*.

Expenses	Cost
Advertising social media, internet ad, community paper, yellow pages, etc. **Field Equipment** label maker and four tapes camera step stool tool kit and materials **Formation and Licensing** business license business registration trademark (optional) **Insurance** **Office Equipment** desk, chair, file cabinet, computer, computer back-up system, printer, scanner, shredder **Marketing Materials** logo design, business card design and printing **Office Supplies** **Professional Development** association membership **Professional Services** accountant, attorney, webmaster	

Expenses	Cost
Telephone **Transportation** **Web Presence** website domain website design package website hosting **TOTAL Start-Up Expenses**	

The following table includes *expenses* professional organizers should consider in their business financial planning for their business *operating costs*.

Expenses	Cost
Advertising Benefits (health insurance, retirement plan) Business license Business registration Field supplies Insurance Office equipment for replacements in future years Office supplies Professional development—membership renewal dues, conferences Professional services—tax planning, legal advice, webmaster Taxes (federal and state) Telephone Transportation Website hosting **TOTAL Operating Expenses**	

Action Plan for Getting Started

Follow this checklist to complete what is necessary *before* working with clients:

Professional Development

- ☐ Obtain education and training in how to start and manage a business, how to work with clients, and a client practicum experience. https://www.instituteprofessionalorganizers.com

- ☐ Read books and organizing blogs.
- ☐ Find a mentor or business coach.

Business Formation

- ☐ Go to your state's website and download their New Business Guide, read it, and take necessary actions.
- ☐ Meet with an accountant to decide on your business entity type.
- ☐ Meet with a small business attorney to form your business entity.
- ☐ Register your business with the state(s) you will be doing business in.
- ☐ Obtain your EIN (federal tax ID number) from https://www.irs.gov.
- ☐ Check local license requirement and obtain your business license(s).
- ☐ Register your business trademark at https://www.uspto.gov/trademark.
- ☐ Name your business.
- ☐ Write your business plan.
- ☐ Obtain business liability insurance.

Set Up Your Office

- ☐ Business phone and voice mail message.
- ☐ Business equipment (desk, chair, file cabinet, computer, computer back-up system, printer, scanner, shredder).

Financial

- ☐ Obtain a business checking account.
- ☐ Set up QuickBooks or other financial record-keeping and invoicing system.
- ☐ Prepare your business start-up and first-year budgets.
- ☐ Set up a merchant account to accept credit cards, such as the Square (https://squareup.com).

Marketing and Branding

- ☐ Write your marketing plan.
- ☐ Create your business brand.
- ☐ Create your company logo and tagline.
- ☐ Design your business cards and purchase.
- ☐ Purchase your website domain.
- ☐ Obtain and set up a business email account.

- ☐ Create your website design or hire a webmaster to create your website.
- ☐ Write your website content.
- ☐ Have professional pictures taken of you for your marketing materials and website.
- ☐ Join a networking group (chamber of commerce, BNI, local NAPO chapter, Rotary)

Doing Business

- ☐ Develop a services and fees agreement.
- ☐ Develop your business policies and processes.
- ☐ Prepare your needs assessment questionnaire.
- ☐ Set up a time-management system to track client sessions.
- ☐ Set up a client relationship management (CRM) system.
- ☐ Identify external resources needed to assist you with your client projects.

Resource Requirements

Technology resource requirements include items such as a computer, phone, and printer. Personnel requirements include employees, associates, and independent contractors. Professional requirements include an accountant, attorney, marketing professional, and webmaster. External requirements are products or services for your clients that must be purchased outside the company.

Key Issues

Isolate key decisions and issues that need immediate or near-term resolution and key issues needing long-term resolution. State the consequences of decision postponement. If you are seeking funding, state specifics of both near and long-term key issues.

Risks (Threats) and Rewards

Summarize the risks of the business and how the risks will be addressed. What rewards do you hope to receive? They can be monetary, personal fulfillment, or both.

SWOT Analysis

This is a powerful technique for identifying *strengths* and *weaknesses* and for examining the *opportunities* and *threats* you face. Used in a personal context, it helps you develop your career in a way that takes best advantage of your talents, abilities, and opportunities.

What makes SWOT particularly powerful is that with a little thought, it can help you uncover opportunities that you are well placed to take advantage of. By understanding your weaknesses, you can manage and eliminate threats that would otherwise catch you unawares.

How to Use the Tool

To complete a SWOT analysis, use the SWOT matrix below and write down answers to the following questions:

Strengths:	Weaknesses:
<ul><li>What do you do well?</li><li>What unique resources can you draw on?</li><li>What do others see as your strengths?</li><li>What advantages (for example, skills, education, or connections) do you have that others don't have?</li><li>What do you do better than anyone else?</li><li>What personal resources do you have access to?</li></ul>	<ul><li>What could you improve?</li><li>What resources are you lacking?</li><li>What should you avoid (due to lack of skills, training, physical limitations, etc.)?</li><li>What are others likely to see as your weaknesses?</li></ul>
Opportunities:	**Threats:**
<ul><li>What good opportunities are open to you?</li><li>What trends could you take advantage of?</li><li>How can you turn your strengths into opportunities?</li><li>What are the interesting trends you are aware of?</li></ul>	<ul><li>What trends could hurt you?</li><li>What is your competition doing?</li><li>What threats do your weaknesses expose you to?</li></ul>

Strengths
Consider this from your own perspective and from the point of view of the people around you. Don't be modest. Be as objective as you can. If you are having any difficulty with this, try writing down a list of your characteristics (see chapter 1).

In looking at your strengths, think about them in relation to the people around you. For example, if you're a great organizer and the people around you are great at organizing, then this is not likely to be a strength in your current role; it is likely to be a necessity or even a threat.

Weaknesses
Again, consider this from a personal and external basis. Do other people perceive weaknesses that you do not see? Do coworkers consistently outperform you in key areas? It is best to be realistic now and face any unpleasant truths as soon as possible.

Opportunities
Useful opportunities can come from such things as changes in technology, markets, your company on both a broad and narrow scale, certification related to your field, social patterns, population profiles, lifestyle changes, or local events.

A useful approach to looking at opportunities is also to look at your strengths and ask yourself whether these open any opportunities. Alternatively, look at your weaknesses and ask yourself whether you could open opportunities by eliminating them.

Threats
What obstacles do you face? What are the people around you doing? Is your job (or the demand for the things you do) changing? Is changing technology threatening your position? Could any of your weaknesses seriously threaten you?

A SWOT matrix is a framework for analyzing your internal strengths and weaknesses and the external opportunities and threats you face. This helps you to focus on your strengths, minimize weaknesses, and take the greatest possible advantage of opportunities available. Carrying out this analysis will often be illuminating—both in terms of pointing out what needs to be done and in putting problems into perspective.

ACTIONS

> ☐ Complete your business plan, including your business financial plan.
> ☐ Perform your SWOT analysis.
> ☐ Start your action list; set goals for completing each task.

CHAPTER 4

Fee Structures—How to Charge for Your Services

Description: Many professional organizers undervalue their services. This chapter covers how to determine a reasonable market rate, earn the income you need to, and communicate your value to clients.

- selling your value
- describing the benefits (value) your client will receive
- hourly fee versus project fee
- initial consultation—fee or free?
- travel fee
- materials fee
- national average
- how to determine your fee
- when and how to give yourself a raise

Selling Your Value

The client needs to understand the value of your services. It's hard for a client to know whether your fee is affordable or reasonable until they have had a chance to understand the value of your services to them. If you charge a dollar an hour but don't produce anything of value, your services are too expensive. If you charge $500 an hour and transform someone's life, they need you, and they need to figure out how they can hire you. A person who sees and understands the value of something and wants it can always figure out a way to make it happen if you can make a case for the value of what you do, and thus you can ask a higher fee.

How to Describe the Benefits (Value) Your Client Will Receive

Feature benefits include:
- You have a proven organizing process.
- You will set up systems that will work.
- You will help your client to pick the right containers.

Functional benefits provide your client with:
- more time
- ability to find things
- financial savings
- more space

Emotional benefits provide your client with:
- peace of mind
- less stress
- control
- confidence
- a sense of calm

Inspirational benefits provide your client with:
- the ability to achieve their goals
- a sense of freedom
- clarity, hope, and possibility
- a sense of empowerment
- increased focus and productivity

Hourly Fee versus Project Fee

Most organizers charge by the hour. Some organizers offer sliding scale rates if a client wants to purchase blocks of hours, similar to a personal trainer. Think carefully about what your time is worth and be careful not to lowball or undercharge your fee just to get the job. If you believe in your worth, your client will too. There may be occasions to charge on a project fee basis—whole house organizing or corporate projects. For projects, you might want to add 15 to 20 percent above your fee to account for additional outside time doing research or shopping and to cover additional time of what you originally estimate.

Packages

Psychologically, people like to think they are getting a deal, especially when they feel they don't have money to spend. Packaging your services by reducing the hourly rate with increased hours purchased is what I'm referring to. However, packages need to be paid for in full upfront. This provides cash flow for your business, and it does something even better: it commits the client to the work. Clients cancelling their sessions at the last minute are a thing of the past because of prepayment.

For example, if your hourly rate is $75 and you typically work in three-hour sessions, you could create the following packages:

- 3 hours = $225 no discount
- 6 hours = $400 ~ 10 percent discount
- 9 hours = $575 ~ 15 percent discount
- 12 hours = $725 ~ 20 percent discount

You can create any combination of packages that works for your business plan. The key is to require prepayment with a stipulation (in your services and fees agreement) that the package expires within a specified period (i.e., ninety days) and is nontransferable.

Initial Consultation and Needs Assessment

Many organizers do not charge for the initial consultation and needs assessment (usually no more than one hour). Others don't charge for a follow-up consultation. I do a pretty thorough complimentary assessment on my website (including uploading pictures of their organizing project) and over the phone when a prospect contacts me. This time spent is for my benefit because I'm assessing the problem areas and gathering information about the person's organizing project and other data to determine if I like them and if we'd be a good fit for each other. I'm fact finding, and this assessment is for my benefit. I'm the one learning, and I'm not giving them information or solutions, so why would they pay for that?

On the other hand, the consultation—what I call the "strategy session"—is something I do charge for, and it happens after we've had a phone conversation. I go into the client's space, already knowing fairly well what I'm walking into because I've spent some time on the phone with the client in advance and they have sent me photographs. The session typically lasts one to two hours. I come in and do a thorough tour of the space, ask a lot of questions, offer verbal suggestions, and in the end, I send them (via email) a comprehensive written Organizing Plan of Action from which to work. They can then choose to implement it themselves or hire me to work with them. The client pays for the consultation because they are learning exactly what they need to do to remedy their situation. If you clarify who is receiving the information and the benefit, then you'll know whether you're doing an assessment or a consultation.

Travel Fee

You might consider charging a travel fee for clients who ask you to come to their home/office that is over X miles or over X time. For example, for travel over sixty minutes round-trip, charge your hourly rate in increments of fifteen minutes using Google maps to calculate the trip time. I don't charge the actual time I'm driving because I could get in a traffic jam, and that is not the client's fault.

Materials Fee

Materials are exclusive of your hourly fee and are reimbursable expenses. Some vendors offer NAPO members discounts. There are also many stores that offer "trade" discounts. You may want to pass this discount on to your client, or you may want to keep the discount and not charge your client the time you spend purchasing the materials. Or, you may want to charge a materials procurement (shopping) fee.

National Average

The best way to determine a fee to charge your clients is to understand what professional organizers in your area are charging for similar services. Do *not* call professional organizers in your area pretending to be a potential client to find out their fee. You can research other professional organizers' websites; many list their fee on their services page. You might research other similar professional services fees, such as a personal trainer, personal chef, and personal or business coach.

Articles Quoting Professional Organizer Fees

- *Newsweek* article "Clean Freaks,"[5] 2004: $50–$200/hr.
- *New York Times* article "A Clutter Too Deep for Mere Bins and Shelves,"[6] January 1, 2008: $60–$100/hr.

---

[5] *Newsweek*, accessed June 12, 2018, http://www.newsweek.com/clean-freaks-129009.
[6] *NY Times*, accessed June 12, 2018, https://www.nytimes.com/2008/01/01/health/01iht-01well.8969298.html.

- *NAPO News* June-July 2005, "Who Are We? Highlights of the 2005 NAPO Membership Survey," $49 to more than $125/hr.

How to Determine Your Fee

When deciding what to charge, use this simple formula. What salary do you need to earn? Think of it as if you were applying for a job with a company. What salary do you need to sustain your lifestyle? Add the cost of benefits, such as vacation, sick days, health and disability insurance, life insurance, and retirement plans.

Add in your operating expenses. This equals the gross annual salary needed.

Next, divide this total by the number of hours you can *realistically* expect to work in a year. Due to holidays, vacation, sick days, professional development, and office time, the typical full-time professional *realistically* bills about fifteen out of twenty working days a month, or 720 hours a year (15 days x 12 months x 4 hours a day).

The result will be the amount you should charge per hour.

It is important to note that you will put in many non-billable hours doing your own administrative and marketing work.

Example
Disclaimer: This is only an example of how the formula calculates and is not a service rate recommendation. This worksheet is not intended to suggest any minimum or maximum rates.

Desired [net] Annual Salary	$36,000.00	$36,000.00
+Operating Expenses (50 percent)	50%	$18,000.00
Total [gross] Annual Salary		$54,000.00
Divided by Hours Worked 720 = Hourly Rate to Charge	720	**$75.00**

When and How to Give Yourself a Raise

Eventually, you'll probably be able to raise your fee as you gain more experience. When you do raise your fee, raise it for past clients as well. For clients you are currently working on a project with, you could charge your new fee for future projects with them.

Final Word on Fees

The client wants choices. Without having a different fee for different services, you need to find a way to provide your client choices. For example: hourly fee with the option of (1) hands-on organizing (will cost more); or (2) a plan (probably the least expensive); or (3) a combination of the two. This gives the client three cost choices without different fees.

ACTIONS

☐ What fee will you charge?
☐ Will you charge by the hour or by the project?
☐ How will you structure your fees?

CHAPTER 5

Business Basics

Office Basics Checklist

Office Space

Office Equipment and Furniture

- ✓ bookshelves
- ✓ comfortable chair
- ✓ computer
- ✓ computer backup
- ✓ desk

- ✓ filing cabinet
- ✓ phone
- ✓ printer (preferably color)
- ✓ scanner (optional)
- ✓ shredder

Software

- ✓ accounting and bookkeeping (such as QuickBooks)
- ✓ contact management (such as Microsoft Outlook)
- ✓ internet browser, email, virus protection, firewall
- ✓ productivity suite (Microsoft Office, Open Office, Apple iWork, etc.)

Record Keeping

- ✓ client files
- ✓ deposits and paid invoices
- ✓ expense receipts
- ✓ tax records
- ✓ time-management system, either paper or electronic

Business Forms

- ✓ assessment questionnaire
- ✓ client appraisal form
- ✓ client intake form (initial client contact checklist)
- ✓ invoices
- ✓ letter of agreement
- ✓ phone log
- ✓ proposals (organizing plan of action)

Filing System (specific to your business)

Supplies

- ✓ three-hole punch
- ✓ binders with dividers
- ✓ calculator
- ✓ hanging folders

- ✓ label maker
- ✓ manila folders

Information Supplies

- ✓ business cards
- ✓ catalogs of organizing products
- ✓ client references
- ✓ letterhead, envelopes
- ✓ listing of your services in a flyer or brochure
- ✓ portfolio
- ✓ presentations
- ✓ resource list (products, websites, donation services, handyperson, etc.)
- ✓ thank-you cards

Field Materials Checklist

Field Materials

- ✓ client file
    - ✓ intake form (initial client contact checklist)
    - ✓ agreement
    - ✓ invoice
    - ✓ proposal (needs assessment and plan of action)
    - ✓ directions/map
- ✓ business cards
- ✓ camera
- ✓ flashlight
- ✓ first aid kit
- ✓ information packet/tip sheets
- ✓ mileage book or app to track mileage
- ✓ stepladder

Tool Box and Kit

Tools of the trade:

- air filter mask
- disinfectant wipes
- furniture moving discs
- hammer
- label maker, extra label tape, batteries
- marking pens (Sharpie)
- paperclips and binder clips
- Ziploc bags of various sizes
- Rubber bands
- scissors
- stapler
- tape measure and laser measure

- Band-Aids
- eraser
- garbage bags
- knife (carton knife)
- latex gloves
- pencils/pens
- pliers
- Post-It notes
- rubber mallet
- screwdrivers
- stapler remover

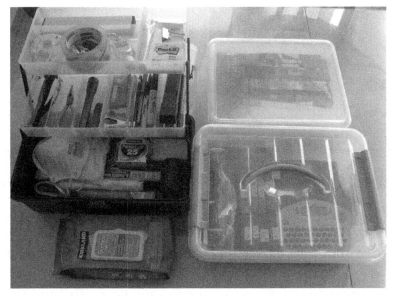

Tools of the trade contained in a hobby box and snap case

Other

- ✓ folding table
- ✓ garment rack
- ✓ hand truck

Paper Management Systems

- ✓ bankers' boxes
- ✓ file labels
- ✓ filing system sample
- ✓ hanging file folders
- ✓ manila file folders
- ✓ plastic file storage boxes

 ACTIONS

☐ Set up your office space with furniture, equipment, and supplies.
☐ Set up your record-keeping systems.
☐ Make a list of resources (handyperson, painter, house cleaner, etc.).
☐ Assemble your tool kit.

CHAPTER 6

Determine Legal and Insurance Needs

Description: This is one of the most critical decisions you will make as a business owner. This chapter will explain the different business entities (United States of America) and help you choose the right one for your situation and goals. The business entities and their advantages and disadvantages that will be discussed are:

- sole proprietorship
- general partnership
- limited liability company (LLC)
- corporation
- S corporation

Also discussed in this chapter is how to register with your state and the federal government, getting insurance for your business, and obtaining licensing.

Disclaimer: This chapter is intended to provide guidance in regard to the subject matter covered. It is provided with the understanding that the author is not herein engaged in rendering legal, accounting, tax, or marketing professional services. If such services are required, professional assistance should be sought.

Registering with State and Federal Governments

To protect your chosen company name, you need to register your company name with the state and federal governments. Also, you protect your personal identity with an EIN. Obtain an employer identification number (EIN) at www.irs.gov/pub/irs-pdf/fss4.pdf by completing the SS-4 Form, Application for Employer Identification Number. There is no cost associated with this application as of this writing.

Registering with your state is done at the state business registry office. For example, in Oregon, register your business at www.filinginoregon.com.

Individuals and sole proprietors would file "Assumed Business Name—New Registration" with the state and include the processing fees and renew annually.

Limited liability companies (LLCs) would file "Articles of Organization—Limited Liability Company" with the state and include the processing fees (varies by state) and renew annually.

Insurance

While business insurance is not generally required, it's a good idea to purchase enough insurance to cover your company's assets. Even if you form a corporation or an LLC, which shields your personal assets from business liabilities, you still risk losing your business if disaster strikes. Insurance can greatly reduce this risk. The two most common and generally useful types of business insurance policies are property insurance and liability insurance.

Permits and Licensing

Check with your local (city, county, etc.) jurisdictions for what may be required.

What Goes into Selecting Your Choice of Business Entity?

Formalities and Expense in Establishing
Sole proprietorships and partnerships are easy to set up. You don't have to file any special forms or pay any fees to start your business. Plus, they don't require you to follow any special operating rules. However, the personal liability risks can outweigh the ease of establishing these entities.

To form an LLC or corporation, you must file a document with the state and pay a fee, which ranges depending on the state where you form your business. Corporations are the most cumbersome to maintain, including electing officers (usually a president, vice president, and secretary) to run the company, and they must keep records of important business decisions and follow other formalities.

Risks and Liabilities
Choosing the right business entity for your business depends largely on the type of services or products it will provide. Even if your business doesn't engage in risky activities—for example, trading stocks or repairing roofs—you'll almost surely want to obtain liability insurance and form a business entity that provides personal liability protection, which shields your personal assets from business debts and claims. This means setting up a corporation or a limited liability company (LLC).

Sole Proprietorship

A sole proprietorship is a business that is owned by *one* person.

Advantages
This is the simplest of business structures to establish and maintain, but you still need to comply with local registration, business license, or permit laws to make your business legitimate. Unlike an LLC or a corporation, you generally don't have to file any special forms or pay any fees to start working as a sole proprietor. All you have to do is declare your business to be a sole proprietorship when you complete the general registration requirements that apply to all new businesses.

In the eyes of the law, a sole proprietorship is not legally separate from the person who owns it. The fact that a sole proprietorship and its owner are one and the same means that a sole proprietor simply reports all business income or losses on his or her individual income tax return, IRS Form 1040 with Schedule C attached. Most cities and many counties require businesses, even tiny home-based sole proprietorships, to register with them and pay at least a minimum tax. In return, your business will receive a business license or tax registration certificate. If you have employees, you need to obtain an employer identification number from the IRS (otherwise your social security number is your employer identification number).

Disadvantages
You are personally responsible for paying both income taxes and business debts. That means that if your business doesn't pay a supplier, defaults on a debt, or loses a lawsuit, the creditor can legally come after your personal property and savings.

As a sole proprietor, you'll have to take responsibility for withholding and paying all income taxes, something an employer would normally do for you. This means paying a self-employment tax, which consists of contributions to Social Security and Medicare, and making payments of estimated taxes throughout the year.

General Partnership

Advantages
You don't have to file any paperwork to establish a general partnership; just agreeing to go into business with another person will get you started. Of course, partnerships must fulfill the same local registration requirements as any new business, such as applying for a business license. Most cities require businesses to register with them

and pay at least a minimum tax. You may also have to obtain an employer identification number from the IRS.

Again, the IRS does not consider partnerships to be separate from their owners for tax purposes. Instead, they are considered "pass-through" tax entities. This means that all of the profits and losses of the partnership "pass through" the business to the partners, who pay taxes on their share of the profits (or deduct their share of the losses) on their individual income tax returns. Each partner's share of profits and losses should be set out in a written partnership agreement.

Disadvantages
Partners are personally liable for all business debts and obligations, including court judgments. This means that if the business itself can't pay a creditor, such as a supplier, lender, or landlord, the creditor can legally come after any partner's house, car, or other possessions.

Corporation

A corporation is an independent legal entity, separate from the people who own, control, and manage it. In other words, corporation and tax laws view the corporation as a legal "person," meaning that the corporation can enter into contracts, incur debts, and pay taxes apart from its owners. A corporation does not dissolve when its owners (shareholders) change or die. The owners of a corporation are not personally responsible for the corporation's debts; this is called limited liability.

Advantages
One of the main advantages of incorporating is that the owners' personal assets are protected from creditors of the corporation. For instance, if a court judgment is entered against your corporation, saying that it owes a creditor $50,000, normally, you can't be forced to use personal assets, such as your house, to pay the debt. Because only corporate assets need be used to pay business debts, you stand to lose only the money that you've invested in the corporation.

Disadvantages
To form a corporation, you must file articles of incorporation with the state corporations division. In addition to filing articles of incorporation, you must create corporate bylaws. While bylaws do not have to be filed with the state, they are important because they set out the basic rules that govern the ongoing formalities and decisions of corporate life, such as how and when to hold regular and special meetings of directors

and shareholders and the number of votes that are necessary to approve corporate decisions.

Finally, you must issue stock certificates to the initial owners (shareholders) of the corporation and record who owns the ownership interests (shares or stock) in the business.

Corporations and their owners must observe certain formalities to retain the corporation's status as a separate entity. Specifically, corporations must:

- hold annual shareholders' and directors' meetings
- keep minutes of shareholders' and directors' major decisions
- make sure that corporate officers and directors sign documents in the name of the corporation
- maintain separate bank accounts from their owners
- keep detailed financial records
- file a separate corporate income tax return

S Corporation

An S corporation is a regular corporation that has elected "S corporation" tax status. An S corporation lets you enjoy the limited liability of a corporate shareholder but pay income taxes on the same basis as a sole proprietor, partner, or LLC.

Advantages
Owners have limited personal liability for business debts. Owners report their share of corporate profit or loss on their personal tax returns. Owners can use corporate loss to offset income from other sources. Fringe benefits can be deducted as business expense.

Disadvantages
It is more expensive to create than a partnership or sole proprietorship. There is more paperwork than for a limited liability company, which offers similar advantages. The income must be allocated to owners according to their ownership interests. The fringe benefits are limited for owners who own more than 2 percent of shares.

Limited Liability Company (LLC)

A limited liability company (LLC) is an ownership structure that is similar to a corporation. Actually, it combines attributes of both corporations and partnerships (or, for one-person LLCs, sole proprietorships). An LLC offers the corporation protection from personal liability for business debts and the pass-through tax structure of partnerships and sole proprietorships. If you're concerned about being held personally liable for debts of your business, then an LLC may be just the thing for you.

Advantages
While LLC owners enjoy limited personal liability for many of their business transactions, it is important to realize that this protection is not absolute. This drawback is not unique to LLCs; however, the same exceptions apply to corporations. An LLC owner can be held personally liable if he or she:

- personally and directly injures someone
- personally guarantees a bank loan or a business debt on which the LLC defaults
- fails to deposit taxes withheld from employees' wages
- intentionally does something fraudulent, illegal, or clearly wrong-headed that causes harm to the company or to someone else
- treats the LLC as an extension of his or her personal affairs, rather than as a separate legal entity

This last exception is the most important. In some circumstances, a court might say that the LLC doesn't really exist and find that its owners are really doing business as individuals, who are personally liable for their acts. To keep this from happening, make sure you and your co-owners:

- Act fairly and legally. Do not conceal or misrepresent material facts or the state of your finances to vendors, creditors, or other outsiders.
- Fund your LLC adequately. Invest enough cash into the business so that your LLC can meet foreseeable expenses and liabilities.
- Keep LLC and personal business separate. Get a federal employer identification number, open up a business-only checking account, and keep your personal finances out of your LLC accounting books.
- Create an operating agreement. Having a formal written operating agreement lends credibility to your LLCs separate existence.
- Always use and state LLC with your business name.

To create an LLC, you begin by filing articles of organization (in some states called a certificate of organization or certificate of formation) with the LLC division of your state government. This office is often in the same department as the corporations division, which is usually part of the secretary of state's office.

You can form an LLC with just one person. While there's no maximum number of owners that an LLC can have, for practical reasons, you'll probably want to keep the group small. An LLC that's actively owned and operated by more than about five people risks problems with maintaining good communication and reaching consensus among the owners.

Many states supply a blank one-page form for the articles of organization, on which you need only specify a few basic details about your LLC, such as its name and address and contact information for a person involved with the LLC (usually called a registered agent) who will receive legal papers on its behalf. Some states also require you to list the names and addresses of the LLC members.

In addition to filing articles of organization, you must create a written LLC operating agreement. While you don't have to file your operating agreement with the state, it's a crucial document because it sets out the LLC members' rights and responsibilities, their percentage interests in the business, and their share of the profits.

Finally, your LLC must fulfill the same local registration requirements as any new business, such as applying for a business license and registering a fictitious or assumed business name.

Disadvantages

It is more expensive to create than a partnership or sole proprietorship because of the attorney fees associated with the preparation of the entity's documents.

 ACTIONS

- ☐ Meet with your accountant and attorney to determine which business entity you should form based on your business model.
- ☐ After you have your business name (read chapter 7 first), register your business with the states you will be doing business in.
- ☐ After you have your business name and business entity documents (articles of incorporation or articles of organization), complete the federal SS-4 form to obtain an EIN number.
- ☐ After you have your EIN number, obtain a business checking account.
- ☐ After you have your business name, apply for business license.

CHAPTER 7

Name and Register Your Business for Maximum Impact

Description: People make an impression in the first two seconds they meet someone. If your name is the first way to introduce yourself to a prospective client, what impression will you make?

- What's in a name?
- What do you want to project?
- What first impression do you want to make?
- How do you search for business names?
- How do you search for internet domain names?
- How do you register your business name?

What's in a Name?

It is how you are viewed by anyone who reads it. They get an instant image of your business and what you do.

What Do You Want to Project?

You want your name to project that you are professional and qualified. What other qualities should it indicate?

First Impressions Do Matter

People get an impression of you within the first two seconds of meeting you. If your business name is their first impression, you need to consider including in your business name information about what you do as a professional organizer.

Be Careful Using Your Own Personal Name

It is getting harder to find a unique name for a professional organizing business. One of the easiest ways to name your business is using your own name or initials plus the word *organizing*, unless you might change your name. For example:

- AMB Organizing Solutions
- AMB Organizing Services
- Organization by Anne
- Organizing with Anne
- Blumer Organizing Services
- Portland Organizer

Names that don't work well because they don't indicate they are in the professional organizing business include:

- Andrews Personal Consulting (Sandra Andrews)
- Busy as a Bea (Bea Baird)
- Ideas in Bloom (Wendy Bloom)
- Options by Ana (Ana Popielnicki)

Names that do work because they indicate the person is a professional organizer include:

- Organize with Kate (Kate Murrell)
- Cheryl's Organizing Concepts (Cheryl Larson)
- Organization by Suzanne (Suzanne Hosea)

More names that do not indicate you are a professional organizer include:
- A Custom Solution
- A to Z Home Management
- Getting Clear
- Timely Living
- Clear the Decks
- Winged Pig

Names that are too cute or misuse words include:

- Organique-Unique

- H/OME (Home/Office Made Easy)
- De-Clutter Bug
- Mind Over Matter (MOM)

Names that indicate exactly what you do include:

- Office Organizers of Houston
- Creative Organizing Solutions
- The Organizing Coach
- Organizing Solutions
- Organizing Resources

Choose Your Name Wisely

You will want your business name to resonate with people you are trying to reach, but don't limit yourself in the event you have future growth:

Limiting: Sally's Kitchen Organizing
Less Limiting: Sally's Organizing

Other Tips
- Keep your name short.
- Answer the phone saying your business name. Can you say it easily?
- Make your name easy to spell.
- Communicate exactly what your business is.

Register Your Business Name

Every time you change your name, you will need to register the new name with the state business registry. You may also incur the expense of reprinting business cards and other promotional and marketing pieces.

- Website domain name registration: Check www.whois.net, www.godaddy.com, or www.networksolutions.com to search if your name is available.
- State business registry: For example, in Oregon go to www.filinginoregon.com.
- Federal registration (optional): Register at www.uspto.gov. This is the US Patent and Trademark Office.

ACTIONS

- ☐ Brainstorm some possible business names. Review and make sure your business name says exactly what you do.
- ☐ If you are a NAPO member, check the NAPO member directory online to see if another professional organizer has your company name in use.
- ☐ Google your business name to see if anything exists under that name.
- ☐ Check to find out if your business name is already a domain or if it is available. If your name is available, purchase your domain; www.whois.net, www.godaddy.com and www.networksolutions.com are popular sites to search and purchase domains.
- ☐ Once you have determined your business entity, register your name with your state business registry. If you form an LLC, it is your business name, LLC. If you form a corporation, it is your business name, Inc.

CHAPTER 8

Tax Issues to Consider and Understand: What You Need to Know to Be Tax Savvy and Tax Benefits You Should Understand

Description: This chapter will guide you through the labyrinth of the United States of America tax details a small and home-based business owner needs to understand and comply with including:

- selecting software to track your business records
- deductions for your home business
- business use of your home
- business use of your automobile
- business travel
- estimated taxes
- payroll taxes
- local taxes and licenses
- filing Form 1099 for professional services

Disclaimer: This chapter is intended to provide guidance in regard to the subject matter covered. It is provided with the understanding that the author is not herein engaged in rendering legal, accounting, tax, or marketing professional services. If such services are required, professional assistance should be sought.

Note: Source of information for this chapter is Julia Fitzgerald, retired CPA, Portland, Oregon. The information in this chapter subject to change.

Software Options for Your Business Records

- Quicken Deluxe

- Quicken Premier
- Quicken Premier Home & Business
- QuickBooks Online
- QuickBooks Simple Start
- QuickBooks Pro
- QuickBooks Premier
- QuickBooks for specific industries
- Websites www.quicken.com and www.intuit.com

Tips on Setting up Quicken or QuickBooks

- Set up the category/account list according to your needs (the shorter the better).
- Set up your filing system according to your category/account names.
- Code transactions consistently.
- Ask questions from an expert.
- Get training if you have never used financial accounting software.
- Reconcile your bank and credit card statements monthly.
- Reconcile your accounts receivable and payables monthly.
- Learn one module at a time.
- If you work with an accountant, have them set up your category/account names. It will save you time and money when they prepare your tax filing.

Deductions for Your Business

- advertising
- car and truck expenses: actual versus mileage
- commissions and fees: services for nonemployees (You must send a 1099 for payments of $600 or more to the same recipient.)
- depreciation: up to $250,000 on new equipment purchased each year
- insurance: liability, malpractice, casualty, overhead, bonds, merchandise and inventory, workers compensation
- health insurance: can deduct 100 percent if you are not eligible for coverage with a group health plan
- interest expense on business note payables
- legal and professional fees
- office expenses
- pension and profit-sharing plans

- rent or lease
- repairs and maintenance
- supplies
- taxes and licenses
- training and education
- travel
- meals and entertainment
- utilities
- telephone
- wages
- professional dues and memberships (except health clubs)
- other expenses

Asset versus Expense

Classify business equipment and furnishings as an asset if it has a life longer than one year and costs greater than $200; otherwise classify as supplies expense. The cost to place the equipment into use is included in the cost—that is, shipping, labor to install, and so on.

Business Use of Home

The business percentages of expenses below are generally deductible on Form 8829:

- mortgage interest
- real estate taxes
- home repairs and maintenance
- water, sewer, garbage
- rent
- utilities (first home line not deductible)
- depreciation
- house insurance
- security system
- casualty losses

Business Percentage

Business percentage of the home is determined by dividing the area *exclusively* used for business by the total area of the home.

- Direct expense: benefits only the business part of the home. One hundred percent of direct expenses are generally deductible against business income.
- Indirect expense: benefits both the business and personal parts of the home. Included are the upkeep and running of the entire home. The business percentages of indirect expenses are generally deductible against business income.
- It is not always the best option to claim a home office for tax purposes. Ask your accountant what is best for your situation.
- To be considered sufficient for a deduction, a home office must meet the following criteria:

    - The office must be a room or part of the home that is used exclusively and regularly for the business.
    - The home must be your principal place of business.
    - The home must be where you meet or deal with clients in the normal course of business.

Sale of the Home

For sales of a personal residence, a homeowner may exclude from income up to $250,000 of gain, and a married couple may exclude up to $500,000 of gain realized on the sale.

Individuals
- Ownership and use: the individual must have owned and used the home as a principal residence for at least two out of the five years prior to the sale (the two years do not have to be consecutive).
- Frequency limitation: the exclusion applies to only one sale every two years.

Married Couples
- Joint return: the married couple must file a joint return.
- Ownership: either or both spouses must have owned the residence for at least two out of the five years prior to the sale.
- Use: both spouses must have used the residence as their principal residence for at least two out of the five years prior to the sale.
- Frequency limitation: neither spouse may have sold a home more than once every two years.

Business Use of Automobile

There are two methods to deduct your vehicle expenses, and it is a good idea to compare their outcomes to determine which one would be best for you.

- Actual costs: deduct the business-use percentage times the actual cost of running the vehicle (depreciation licenses, lease payments, registration fees, gas, insurance, repairs, oil, garage rent, tires, tolls, parking fees).
- If you use your car for both business and personal purposes, you must divide your expenses between business and personal use.
- Standard mileage: deduct the standard mileage rate, which includes all vehicle costs except business parking and tolls, the business percentage of interest paid on a vehicle loan, and the business percentage of personal property taxes paid on the vehicle. Depreciation is included in the cents per mile deduction.
- Refer to IRS publication 463 for additional information.

Business Travel

Elements to prove business travel expenses include:

- Amount: amount of each separate expense for travel, lodging, and meals.
- Time: date left and returned for trip and number of days for business.
- Place: name of city or other designation.
- Business purpose: business reason for travel or the business benefit gained or expected to be gained.

Deductibility of travel expenses include:

- transportation and lodging: 100 percent
- meals while away from home: 50 percent
- cost of conference/seminar: 100 percent

Types of expenditures include:

- Transportation: travel by airplane, train, bus, or car between home and business destination. If the ticket is provided or free as a result of a frequent traveler or similar program, the cost is zero.

- Commuter bus, taxi, airport limousine: fares for transportation to or from airport or station and the hotel, and hotel and location of the business meeting place.
- Car: operating and maintaining a car when traveling away from home on business. Deduct actual expenses or the standard mileage rate, including business-related tolls and parking.
- Lodging and meals: lodging and meals if the business trip is overnight or long enough to require a stop for sleep. Cost of meals includes amounts spent for food, beverages, taxes, and related tips.
- Cleaning: dry cleaning and laundry.
- Telephone: business calls on a business trip. Includes business communication by fax machine or other communication devices.
- Refer to IRS publication 463 for additional information.

Business versus Personal Travel Expenses

- Entirely for business: all travel expenses are deductible.
- Primarily for business: deductible travel expenses include the travel costs of getting to and from the business destination, and any business-related expenses at the business destination. (Nonbusiness side trips are not deductible.) Whether a trip is primarily business or personal depends on the facts and circumstances of each case. The amount of time during the trip spent on personal activity compared to the amount of time spent on activities directly relating to business is an important factor in determining whether the trip is primarily personal.
- Primarily for personal reasons: the entire cost of the trip is nondeductible. However, any business-related expenses incurred at the destination are deductible.
- Refer to IRS publication 463 for additional information.

Estimated Taxes

The general rule for estimated tax payments is to pay in 100 percent of last year's total tax or 90 percent of this year's total tax. Divide the total into four payments to be paid each quarter by the due date.

- April 15—first payment due
- June 15—second payment due

- September 15—third payment due
- January 15—fourth payment due

To electronically pay all your taxes, go to www.eftps.gov and enroll. Pay your taxes more often than four times. For cash flow, pay something each month toward your estimated taxes.

Payroll Taxes

Federal Forms
- Form 941 Employers Quarterly Federal Tax Return: due each quarter by the end of the month following the quarter (e.g., first quarter due by April 30).
- Form 940 Employers: due by January 30 for the previous year's payroll.
- Form 944 Employers Annual Federal Tax Return: due by January 31 for the previous year's payroll.
- Form W-2 Employee Wage statements: due to recipients by January 30 for the previous year's payroll.
- Form 1099 Misc: due to the recipients by January 30 for the previous year's nonemployee compensation. Must send one to each unincorporated individual or business for payments of $600 or greater.

State Forms (Oregon as an example)
- Form OQ Oregon Combined Quarterly Tax Report: due each quarter by the end of the month following the quarter.
- Form WR Oregon Annual Withholding Tax Reconciliation Report.

Local Taxes (Oregon as an example)
- Personal Property Tax: due March 1 of each year for previous calendar year. Tax is paid on value of equipment and furniture that business has accumulated since inception.
- TriMet and LTD Transit District Self-Employment Taxes (Oregon): due April 15 of each year. This income tax is applied to self-employment earnings of taxpayers doing business, or providing services, within the district that are not subject to payroll tax.
- Combined Report Form (Oregon): Portland City Business License-Multnomah County Business Income Tax. To check rates, go to the Portland, Oregon Bureau of Licenses website is www.pdxbl.org.

Filing Form 1099

Form 1099-Misc is required to be filed for each person the business pays professional fees of $600 or more in a calendar year. The 1099s must be furnished to the recipients by February 1 of each year for the previous calendar year's activity. A Form 1096 must accompany the 1099 that is sent to the government.

ACTIONS

- ☐ Select and set up software or other financial record-keeping system to track income and deductions for your business.
- ☐ Select and set up a payroll service for your business.
- ☐ Decide if you will use actual costs or standard mileage for business use of automobile.
- ☐ Complete appropriate referenced forms for your business model and entity.

CHAPTER 9

Marketing and Branding Your Organizing Business and How to Find Clients

Description: This chapter covers how to create a brand for yourself, how to create a winning marketing message and successful marketing approaches, how to develop your network for long-term success, and how to create a successful website.

- creating your brand
- writing a winning marketing message
- communicating your value
- creating your elevator speech
- how to find clients
  - developing your network of strategic alliances
  - developing a successful website
  - five steps to creating a blog with Google
  - thirty-minute formula
  - one hundred marketing approaches

What Is the Difference between Marketing, Advertising, and Public Relations?

The following quote is attributed to M. Booth and Associates, Inc. as taken from a *Reader's Digest* story called "Promoting Issues and Ideas": "If the circus is coming to town, and you paint a sign saying, 'Circus coming to the fairgrounds Saturday,' that's *advertising*. If you put the sign on the back of an elephant and walk him into town, that's *promotion*. If the elephant walks through the mayor's flowerbed, that's *publicity*. If you can get the mayor to laugh about it, that's *public relations*, and if you actually planned the elephant's walk, that's *marketing*."

Creating Your Brand

A brand is more than a logo. A brand means being known. A brand is about recognition. You want clients to recognize, respond, and remember you! A brand is the promise of an experience. Your brand should include what experience you want your clients to have with you. Refer to the benefits (value) you provide your clients:

- empowered
- in control
- attain goals
- achievable results
- peace of mind
- more time
- fun
- simple

You need to capitalize on *your* strengths. What is *your* promise of an experience?

For example, with SolutionsForYou—I have the solutions, I can solve their problems, and I am confident that I can provide solutions that will work for them.

It is not a brand unless it is remarkable. You must stand out from everyone else in your line of business. How will you stand out from your competitors?

Writing a Winning Marketing Message and Communicating Your Value

A marketing message is comprised of five elements:

1. Positioning idea: your key marketing message. It is similar to a tagline.
2. Position description: expansion of your marketing message. It is similar to your mission statement.
3. Key messages: no more than three. Pull them from your position description.
4. Supporting details: expansion of your key messages.
5. Key benefits: what your client gains (the value/benefits you give them).

Here is an example of a marketing message:

Institute for Professional Organizers™ Marketing Message

Positioning Idea: The global market leader in Professional Organizing Business Owner Training

Positioning Description: The Institute for Professional Organizers™ is the leading global provider of both business development and professional organizer client engagement training that enable Professional Organizers to attract their key client, increase their confidence, and manage their business through the knowledge, skills, systems, tools, expertise, experience, and continuous support provided by Certified Professional Organizers via live seminars, state-of-the-art webinars, or individual coaching, mentoring, and self-study.

Key Messages	Attract More Key Clients	Manage Your PO Business	Multiple Training Venues
Messaging	Learn how to develop a marketing message and plan to attract your key client	Provide the tools and expertise for participants to successfully start, run, and manage a business specific to the professional organizer industry	Provide the knowledge, skills, systems, tools, experience, certification, and continuous support needed to work with clients specific to the professional
Supporting Details	•Introduction and awareness of key client and specialized services •Identification of key client and services •Research and write a business plan supporting key client market •Marketing and branding methodology and techniques to attract key client •Tools and support (web development) to market participants' business to their key client	•Understanding the professional organizer industry associations and credentials •Provide a detailed action plan and mentoring to implement participants' professional organizing business •Provide tax, legal and insurance knowledge to the Professional Organizer Industry	•Live seminar with hands-on client practicum, certification, and continuous support •State-of-the art webinar training with continuous support •Individual coaching, mentoring, and self-study

Key Messages	Attract More Key Clients	Manage Your PO Business	Multiple Training Venues
Key Benefits	Business is positioned in the market to attract key client	Positioned for stability and growth	Continuous training is financially and geographically achievable

Creating Your Elevator Speech

Why do you need one? It is your answer to, "What do you do?" You want a clear, concise, and valuable message. This is your chance to attract potential clients and stand out from your competitors. Who needs your services, and are you talking to them? You want to be perceived as credible, competent, and professional. You want to be remembered, so don't be boring.

The Formula
Keep it short. Elements to include when creating your own speech include:

1. What you *do*
2. Who you *serve*
3. What your clients *need*
4. What your clients really *want*

Examples:

I organize professionals to be productive and successful.
What I do: organizing
Who I serve: professionals
What my clients need: to be productive
What my clients want: successful

I implement systems for families to simplify their routines and spaces to allow for more family time.

What I do: implement systems
Who I serve: families
What my clients need: simplify routines and spaces
What my clients want: family time

Now when they say, "Tell me more," you need to be able to explain the details of what you do. Now it is about you and how you can provide the solutions they need. Prepare a follow-up to your elevator speech for various audiences.

How to Find Clients

As I mentioned in the Preface, I spent my first six months in business planning and launching. One day, my husband and I were in our office with our desks back to back, and he turned around, kicked my chair, and said, "Don't you think it's about time to get a client?"

I wasn't even sure how to go about finding clients, and our website was not on page 1 of the search listing, so if anyone was looking for a professional organizer, they would not find me. Remember, this was 2003, and professional organizers were not commonplace. The TV shows that have promoted our industry were just beginning.

I asked my husband, "How should I go about finding clients?" He suggested I ask a few friends who had encouraged me if they knew of anyone whose home was a bit cluttered. I pulled together a brochure of my business services and proceeded to meet with everyone I knew, asking them to help me find clients.

This exercised proved to be very worthwhile on two counts: First, I was referred by one of my friends to her client, and I had my first organizing job. Second, I made connections with people who have businesses with clients who need my services, and eventually my clients might need their services. For example, one friend is a financial advisor, and her clients needed help pulling together paper information the financial advisor needs to advise them on. My clients often ask me if I know of a financial advisor because they need to get their finances in order or want to start investing for their retirement. It's a win-win relationship and what is known as a strategic alliance.

Developing Your Network of Strategic Alliances

Strategic alliances are individuals or businesses that share similar clients with you. Network every day. Talk to everyone about your business. Who do you know that can help you promote your business? Who can you partner with and strategically align yourself with to provide mutual marketing opportunities?

Strategic alliance examples include:

- realtors
- interior designers
- schools

- doctors
- lawyers
- certified public accountants
- senior living residences
- financial investment representatives
- feng shui consultants
- wardrobe consultants
- cleaning services

Invite them to meet with you, explain your services, and then ask them, "How can I be of service to you," and watch the flood of referrals come your way. And you will be more valuable to your clients because you have resources for them.

Another way to meet strategic partners is to join networking organizations. Business Networking International is one networking organization I belonged to. They have over 200,000 members. I met many business owners. We exchanged referrals, and I grew my list of trusted resources. Other networking organizations include chambers of commerce, Rotary, small-business associations, Toast Masters, LeTip, I Take the Lead, and Meet-up.

Developing a Successful Website

Include in your website design your company colors, logo, tagline, and font as they all communicate your brand. Websites generally consist of the following pages:

- **Home**: where you communicate to your ideal client your marketing message.
- **About**: a bio about you—your background, how you became a professional organizer, your education and training, your organizing philosophy, your credentials and memberships.
- **Contact**: your company phone number, email, needs assessment form.
- **Services**: what you will provide and what the client will receive (value and benefits).

Additional pages might consist of:

- **Approach**: how to work with a professional organizer.
- **Before/After pictures**: samples of client projects. Include how long it took, both your time and client time, materials used, cost and resources, what their before state was, what their goals were, and what the outcome is.

- **Resources**: a listing of services that your clients can benefit from (i.e., your strategic alliances, donation resources, product resources, etc.).
- **Newsletter or blog**
- **Frequently Asked Questions** (FAQs)

Other information to disclose might include:

- privacy statement
- webmaster information or link to their website
- copyright protection

Website Don'ts

- Do not copy content from another website.
- Do not use photos without a license for them.
- Do not post information about your clients without their permission in writing.

Ways to optimize your website include:

- Submit your site to search engines (Google, Yahoo, MSN, etc.).
- Adding keywords: Google AdWords Keyword Tool is free, and it tells you how many people are searching for each keyword phrase as well as the level of competition. Some examples of keywords you might include are: professional organizer, your city, your state, company name, organizing services, residential organizing, and business organizing. To locate a website's title, keywords, description, and other coding information, right click on the website page and select "view source."
- Description: this is what appears with your website listing when someone does a search for related terms in a search engine. For example, the description for the home page of the Institute for Professional Organizers website is: Institute for Professional Organizers: Become a **Professional Organizer** with our comprehensive and affordable Fast Track Method™ **training** program taught by Certified **Professional Organizer** Anne Blumer.

> Institute for Professional Organizers™ | Become a Professional ...
> www.instituteprofessionalorganizers.com/ ▼
> Become a **Professional Organizer** with our comprehensive and affordable Fast Track Method™ **training** program taught by Certified **Professional Organizer** Anne Blumer.

Five Steps to Creating a Blog with Google

A blog is a medium for you to communicate with clients and prospective clients on an ongoing basis. This is different from a newsletter you distribute on a regular basis. You can provide organizing tips, inspiration, resources, and anything else that will provide value to your key clients—thereby increasing your value. For an example, visit www.solutionsforyouorganizing.blogspot.com.

A blog is simple to create with Google. Follow these steps:

1. Create a Google account. Go to www.Google.com. Sign in if you have a Google account. Otherwise create a Google account. Select "blogger."
2. Name your blog.
3. Choose a template. You can easily change your template any time.
4. Adjust your settings and layout. This is where you format how your blog page will appear and what access you give. This includes:
   - page elements
   - font and colors
   - edit HTML
   - edit template
   - change title
   - add description
   - add your blog to Google's listings
   - let search engines find your blog
   - show quick editing on your blog
   - show email post links
5. Post your first blog entry and post regularly thereafter.

Thirty-Minute Marketing Formula[7]

Every day spend the first thirty minutes:

1. Reviewing your marketing plan
2. Reviewing your financials
3. Looking at your calendar. Is it moving you forward? Is it full? If not, what can you do to generate business?
4. Focusing on your business and getting inspiration
5. Brainstorming

---

[7] Free Report: How to Double Your Business in 30 Days, accessed 2009, www.veronikanoize.com

6. Reading an article about organizing or running a business
7. Making five good karma calls just to say, "Hello, I'm thinking of you" or to compliment someone. The point is to connect with people because *marketing is relationships.*

Top Ten Marketing Approaches

1. **Website:** you can develop your own at www.godaddy.com, www.vistaprints.com or www.weebly.com, to name a few.
2. **Business cards:** you can craft your own at www.vistaprints.com.
3. **Social media:** set up accounts and post regularly on Facebook, Pinterest, Twitter, Instagram, LinkedIn, and Houzz, to name a few.
4. **Networking:** check out as many networking organizations as you can and then decide which ones are a good fit for you and your business. A few to consider are the chamber of commerce, Business Networking International, Entrepreneur Meet-up Groups, Business Alliances, Rotary, and Kiwanis.
5. **Newsletter** (see handouts for monthly examples)

There are a variety of ways you can create and distribute your newsletter. Some options are:
- Send your newsletter with www.constantcontact.com or www.mailchimp.com.
- For a more professional look and feel than a Word document, create your newsletter using Microsoft Publisher and attach it to an email in pdf format.
- Post it in a blog.
- Send it via postal mail.
- Content ideas:
- introduction: a theme for the month (such as Back to School Organizing for the September newsletter)
- tip of the month
- featured product
- client success story (feature one of your client projects along with before/after pictures)
- featured professional resource (feature one of your strategic alliances and how they can help your clients)

6. **Presentations** on topics such as time, paper, and space management (see chapters 15, 16, and 17 for content ideas).
7. **Gift certificates**
8. **Removable car sign:** www.fastsigns.com

9. **Silent auctions**
10. **Seasonal greeting cards:** www.sendoutcards.com

One Hundred Marketing Approaches[8]

General Ideas
1. Never let a day pass without engaging in at least one marketing activity (see thirty-minute marketing formula).
2. Determine a percentage of gross income to spend annually on marketing.
3. Set specific marketing goals every year. Review and adjust quarterly.
4. Maintain a system of marketing ideas for later use.
5. Carry business cards with you (all day, every day).
6. Create a personal nametag or pin with your company name and logo on it and wear it at high-visibility meetings.

Target Market
7. Stay alert to trends that might impact your target market, product, or promotion strategy.
8. Read market research studies about your profession, industry, product, target market groups, etc.
9. Collect competitors' ads and literature. Study them for information about strategy, product features, benefits, etc.
10. Ask clients why they hired you and solicit suggestions for improvement.
11. Ask former clients why they left you.
12. Identify a new market.
13. Join a list-serve (e-mail list) related to your profession.
14. Subscribe to a list-serve or blog that serves your target market.

Networking and Word of Mouth
15. Join a chamber of commerce or other organization.
16. Join or organize a breakfast club with other professionals (not in your field) to discuss business and network referrals.
17. Mail a brochure to members of organizations to which you belong.
18. Send letters to attendees after you attend a conference.
19. Join a community list-serve (e-mail list) on the Internet.

---

[8] Vickys Virtual Office, accessed April 2008, www.vickysvirtualoffice.com, rewritten by the author specifically for the professional organizer industry.

Product Development
20. Create a new service, technique, or product.
21. Offer a simpler/cheaper/smaller version of your (or existing) product or service.
22. Offer a fancier/more expensive/faster/bigger version of your (or existing) product or service.
23. Update your services.

Education, Resources, and Information
24. Establish a marketing and public relations advisory and referral team composed of your colleagues and/or neighboring business owners, share ideas and referrals, and discuss community issues. Meet quarterly for breakfast.
25. Attend a marketing seminar.
26. Read a marketing book.
27. Subscribe to a marketing newsletter or other publication.
28. Subscribe to a marketing list-serve on the Internet.
29. Subscribe to a marketing blog.
30. Train your clients and colleagues to promote referrals.
31. Hold a monthly marketing meeting with employees or associates to discuss strategy and status and solicit marketing ideas.
32. Join an association or organization related to your profession.
33. Get a marketing intern to take you on as a client. It will give the intern experience and you some free marketing help.
34. Maintain a consultant card file for finding designers, writers, and other marketing professionals. Hire a marketing consultant to brainstorm with.

Pricing and Payment
35. Analyze your fee structure and look for areas requiring modifications or adjustments.
36. Establish a credit card payment option for clients.
37. Learn to barter and offer discounts to members of certain clubs/professional groups/organizations in exchange for promotions in their publications.
38. Give quick pay or cash discounts.
39. Offer financing or installment plans.

Marketing Communications
40. Publish a newsletter for customers and prospects (it doesn't have to be fancy or expensive).
41. Develop a brochure of services.

42. Remember, business cards aren't working for you if they're in the box. Pass them out! Give prospects two business cards and brochures—one to keep and one to pass along.
43. Create a calendar to give away to customers and prospects.
44. Print a tagline and/or one-sentence description of your business on letterhead, fax cover sheets, and invoices.
45. Develop a site on the World Wide Web.
46. Create a signature file to be used for all your e-mail messages. It should contain contact details, including your website address and key information about your company that will make the reader want to contact you.
47. Include testimonials from customers in your literature and on your website.

Media Relations
48. Update your media list often so that press releases are sent to the right media outlet and person.
49. Write a column for the local newspaper, local business journal, or trade publication.
50. Publish an article and circulate reprints.
51. Send timely and newsworthy press releases as often as needed.
52. Get public relations and media training or read up on it.
53. Appear on a radio or TV talk show.
54. Write a letter to the editor of your local newspaper or trade magazine.
55. Get a publicity photo taken and enclose with press releases.
56. Consistently review newspapers and magazines for possible PR opportunities.
57. Submit tip articles to newsletters, e-zines (An e-zine is a periodic publication distributed by email or posted on a website. E-zines are typically tightly focused on a subject area), and newspapers.
58. Conduct industry research and develop a press release or article to announce an important discovery in your field.
59. Create a media kit and keep its contents current.

Customer Service and Customer Relations
60. Return phone calls promptly.
61. Record a memorable message or tip of the day on your outgoing answering machine or voice mail message.
62. Ask clients what you can do the help them.
63. Take clients out to a ball game, show, or another special event—just send them two tickets with a note. Hold a seminar at your office for clients and prospects.

64. Send handwritten thank-you notes.
65. Send birthday cards and appropriate seasonal greetings. See www.sendoutcards.com.
66. Photocopy interesting articles and send them to clients and prospects with a handwritten FYI note and your business card.
67. Send a book of interest or other appropriate business gift to a client with a handwritten note.
68. Create an area on your website specifically for your customers.

Advertising
69. Get a memorable phone number, such as 1-800-ORGANIZ.
70. Provide Rolodex® cards or phone stickers preprinted with your business contact information.
71. Promote your business jointly with other professionals via cooperative direct mail.
72. Advertise in a specialty directory or in the yellow pages.
73. Write an ad in another language to reach the non-English-speaking market. Place the ad in a publication that your market reads, such as in a Hispanic newspaper.
74. Distribute advertising specialty products such as pens, mouse pads, or mugs.
75. Mail bumps—photos, samples, and other innovative items to your prospect list. (A bump is simply anything that makes the mailing envelope bulge and makes the recipient curious about what's in the envelope!)
76. Create a direct-mail list of hot prospects.
77. Consider nontraditional tactics such as bus backs, billboards, and popular websites.
78. Consider a vanity automobile tag with your company name. See www.fastsigns.com.
79. Create a friendly bumper sticker for your car.
80. Code your ads and keep records of results to analyze effectiveness.
81. Create a new or improved company logo or recolor the traditional logo.
82. Sponsor and promote a contest or sweepstakes during GO Month (January).

Special Events and Outreach
83. Get a booth at a fair/trade show attended by your target market.
84. Give a speech or volunteer for a career day at a high school.
85. Teach a class or seminar at a local college or adult education center.

86. Sponsor an Adopt-a-Road area in your community to keep roads litter free. People that pass by the area will see your name on the sign announcing your sponsorship.
87. Volunteer your time to a charity or nonprofit organization.
88. Donate your product or service to a charity auction.
89. Appear on a panel at a professional seminar.
90. Write a how-to pamphlet or article for publishing.
91. Produce and distribute an educational video.
92. Publish a book or an e-book. See www.lulu.com.

Sales Ideas

93. Start every day with two cold or follow-up calls.
94. Read newspapers, business journals, and trade publications for new business openings, personnel appointments, and promotion announcements made by companies. Send your business literature to appropriate individuals and firms.
95. Give your sales literature to your lawyer, accountant, printer, banker, temp agency, office supply salesperson, advertising agency, etc. (Expand your sales force for free!)
96. Follow up on your direct mailings, e-mail messages, and broadcast faxes with a friendly telephone call.
97. Try using e-mail delivery instead of direct mail. (e-mail, allows you to send the same message to many contacts at once.) See www.constantcontact.com or www.mailchimp.com
98. Use broadcast faxes or e-mail messages to notify your customers of product service updates.
99. Extend your hours of operation.
100. Call and/or send mail to former clients to try and reactivate them.

First-Year Marketing Plan

With all the information laid out above, it is now time for you to craft your marketing plan.

Identify and list your *first-year* top five marketing strategy goals and three objectives for each. Prioritize each goal using 1–5. Assign a deadline for each objective. For example:

Priority Rank 1–5	Goals	Objectives	Deadline
1	Build website	Hire a webmaster Write content Launch site	July 1 August 1 August 15
2	Develop strategic alliances/power partners	Identify alliances Contact alliances, introduce, invite to meet Meet with alliances	August 1 August 7 August 31
3	Speak to three groups this year	Identify twelve groups to speak to Contact groups Book three presentations	September 1 September 15 October 15
4	Deliver monthly newsletters	Develop initial contact data base Write newsletter Send newsletter and track traffic	October 1 October 5 October 15
5	Create social media presence	Create LinkedIn account Connect with one new person each day Post events/workshops	November 1 Ongoing Ongoing

ACTIONS

- ☐ Craft your marketing message.
- ☐ Prepare your elevator speech.
- ☐ Write content for your website.
- ☐ Research other professional organizer websites.
- ☐ Create a blog.
- ☐ Do at least one of the one hundred marketing ideas each week.
- ☐ Call five people and practice making karma calls.
- ☐ Craft your marketing plan for your first year in business.

PART II

The Client Process

CHAPTER 10

Client Process —Phase 1: Connecting with the Client

Description: The initial client contact is the first of the three phases of the client process. This chapter covers the first phase—connecting with the client.

Client Process

The client process consists of three distinct phases: connecting with the client, client needs assessment, and completing the client project.

The majority of your clients will contact you initially by phone. Being prepared for when your client calls will help portray you as a professional.

Points to Consider to Prepare You for When Your Client Calls

- What is your objective?
- How do you want to be perceived?
- Be professional.
- Have a professional-sounding voicemail message.
- Train your family members to answer your phone or have a separate phone line for your business.
- Would you want to work with you after hearing you talk?

The First Five Questions to Ask

To save you unnecessary time explaining your process and fees, ask the following questions first to filter out any clients you do not want to work with because of location, what needs to be organized, personal concerns, or your availability:

1. What is their location? Is it within your working radius? If not, you may want to pass the opportunity on to another professional organizer.
2. What is their time frame for getting the job done? If you are not available during that time, you can let them know, and they may have more flexibility.
3. What area(s) need organizing? If it is an area you are not skilled in or prefer not to organize, you may want to pass the opportunity on to another professional organizer.
4. What pets do they have? If you are allergic to certain pets or are not comfortable around certain animals, you may want to pass the opportunity on to another professional organizer, or you may ask that the pets are not present when you are working with a client.
5. Are they a smoker? If you are sensitive to cigarette smoke or odors, you may want to pass this opportunity on to another professional organizer, or you can request that clients not smoke when you are present.

Developing Your Thirty-Second Hook

You must be prepared to succinctly talk about your business and how you can help the client. Your hook should include the following:

- your fees
- confidential services
- your credibility

- how you work or your process
- benefits of working with you

Example

"You can expect complete confidentiality, and I adhere to the National Association of Productivity & Organizing Professionals' code of ethics. I work with my clients in three phases.

"The first phase is a complimentary needs assessment to define your goals and schedule organizing sessions for the second phase. The second phase is the implementation of my organizing process. My rate for phase two sessions is $X/hour. The implementation can be accomplished by working with you hands-on, providing side-by-side assistance. Or, I can work with you by coaching, providing you with assignments to complete on your own between our consultations. The third phase is a thirty-minute complimentary evaluation appointment to ensure your organizing systems are working for you.

"The benefits you will receive from my services might include more time and space, saving money, improved relationships, less stress, and increased productivity and focus. Doesn't that sound great?

"When is the best time to schedule your complimentary needs assessment?"

What You Need to Know from Your Client—Closing the Conversation

Have your questions in front of you. You need as much of a visual of their organizing need as you can obtain from them before you decide you even want to work with them. At a minimum, ask these questions:

- How did they hear about you?
- Is the organizing for the person contacting you or someone else? Who else will be involved in the organizing project?
- Do they want hands-on help or advice?
- Is the problem in one room of the house or the entire house (or building, office, etc.)?
- How long has the problem been going on?
- What is their organizing budget?
- When can they start?
- Ask for directions to their location. Don't rely on a web-based mapping tool; they are not always reliable.

- Ask for their home/business/mobile phone numbers.
- Ask for their email address.

Use this time to qualify your clients and decide if you're a good match for each other. Listen carefully to hear how they are feeling. Then repeat back to them what you're hearing. For example, you might say, "It sounds like you're feeling overwhelmed about how to get started." You'll appear empathetic and approachable.

You Have a Consultation Scheduled—What's Next?

- Schedule your consultation for no more than an hour if you are not charging for it.
- Record the consultation (time/date and client information) in your time management tool.
- Enter the client information in your contacts database.
- Email a confirmation of the needs assessment session date and time to your client along with any additional information you want to provide at this point.

Preparing for the Needs Assessment

Prepare and take with you a client file, including:

- Client folder, including:
    - intake form
    - map (directions) to client
    - client needs assessment questionnaire
    - organizing plan of action template
    - letter of agreement (The letter of agreement along with a confirmation of your initial session can be sent via email prior to your session. Alternatively, you could send the letter of agreement through DocuSign and have it signed prior to your consultation.)
    - invoice for needs assessment (If charging. Alternatively, you could send an invoice for prepayment of the assessment session through QuickBooks, PayPal, or a scheduling app such as Schedulicity.)
- your workbag with your camera and tape measure at a minimum
- business cards
- a bottle of water
- confidence and energy

Checklists

See the Forms section in appendix A for the checklists and the client intake form to use during each of the phases of the client process, to help you be prepared.

 EXERCISES

- Write your thirty-second hook.
- Prepare a list of questions you will ask when someone calls.

CHAPTER 11

Client Process—Phase 2: How to Effectively Conduct a Needs Assessment and Scheduling the Project

Description: The needs assessment discoveries will be your road map to clearly identifying your client's goals, needs, barriers, and expectations. This chapter will provide you with questions to ask your client that will help you best assess their organizing needs and, from there, develop an organizing plan of action.

- how to conduct an assessment without giving away too much information
- environmental issues needs—assessment questions
- emotional issues needs—assessment questions
- expectation needs—assessment questions
- scheduling the project

Overview

The needs assessment is a tool and process for you to gather information about what the client needs and how you can help them (or not). It can be conducted on the phone, in email form, by completing an online form, or in person.

If you are conducting the needs assessment in person and *not charging* for it, you don't want to tell the potential client how you are going to help them. Otherwise, they will take all of your useful information and decide to try to do it themselves. Your time is valuable, so limit your in-person needs assessment to less than an hour if you are not charging for it.

If you are charging for the needs assessment, you can promote it as an "organizing plan of action," where you meet with the client in their environment and conduct the needs assessment but also provide a few ideas that you will incorporate into an overall organizing plan of action. They can then implement it on their own, you can work with them to implement it, or you can implement the plan for them. This approach can be done by charging for a one-hour in-person assessment followed by charging a minimum of one hour for plan development.

If the client has not been disorganized their entire adult life, then usually something happened that caused a change in their life, and their organization systems stopped functioning. This is called "situational disorganization." Some possible causes of situational disorganization are:

- Someone was born, or someone died.
- They moved or changed jobs.
- The children moved out or back in.
- They are marrying or divorcing.
- Their hobbies are taking over the environment.
- They are creating a home-based business.
- They are selling or buying a home.
- They are downsizing.
- There is a medical condition or aging issues.

What to Expect

Plan to arrive ten to fifteen minutes in advance of your scheduled time. Traffic can be unpredictable, and this gives you a cushion to ensure you are on time. One morning, I was on my way to my client's organizing session, and the traffic on the freeway was at a standstill. I called my client to let her know I would be delayed, and she replied, "If you can't show up on time, don't bother!"

Also, with that ten to fifteen minutes' cushion, if you arrive early, take a few minutes in the comfort of your car or at a nearby coffee shop to review your client's intake form, take a few deep cleansing breaths, let go of other distractions, and get focused on your client.

Knock on your client's door and get a warm smile on your face. Introduce yourself and let them know how happy you are to be there. Your client is probably a bit anxious and uncertain about what to expect, so your first task is to put them at ease. They typically will say, "I don't know how this works. Should I show you the room I want help with or should we sit down first?" I like to sit down first. It helps the client get grounded with me and gives me a chance to take in the client's environment. Your client may offer you a beverage, and you can graciously decline, stating you brought water for yourself. This lets them know that you are there to serve and support them, not the other way around.

This would be a good time to review with your client their goals in working with you. From there, ask if you can have a tour of the environment with your client. Listen to what the client is saying but observe everything. Listen for how they speak. Do they sound sad, happy, angry, confused, overwhelmed, anxious, or frustrated?

Conducting the Needs Assessment

The needs assessment discoveries will be your road map to clearly identifying your client's goals, needs, barriers, and expectations.

During the assessment, you may want to look in drawers, behind cabinet doors, and in closets. Before opening drawers, ask permission first by saying, "May I look inside this drawer/closet/cabinet?"

Ask your client the following questions and those found on the needs assessment forms (residential or business) located in the Forms section (see appendix A) or observe the environment for your answers to these questions.

Environmental Questions
1. What specifically is not working for you?
2. Am I organizing your paper, space, or time?
3. What is working?
4. What is the function of each room—or how would you like each space to function? (List each room they want you to work in.)
5. Is there too much stuff or not enough storage? Or a combination of both?
6. Which family members will be working with us, and is everyone agreeable to go through this process?
7. Do you prefer things to be out in view or put away out of sight?
8. What is your vision for this space?
9. What are your goals for this space?

Emotional Questions
1. Why do you want to get organized?
   Responses you might hear include:
   - I'm tired of living this way.
   - I can't find what I need when I need it.
   - I want to be a good role model to my children.
   - I want to be more successful in my job.
   - I'm embarrassed to have friends over.

- I'm feeling out of control.
- I don't want to continue spending money on items I already have but can't find.

2. What do you think are your barriers?
   Responses you might hear include:
   - My husband/wife is a slob.
   - My children expect me to pick up after them all the time.
   - I'm too busy with my job to keep the house organized.
   - I don't feel well.
   - I'm really tired all the time.
   - There is no place to put anything; nothing makes sense to me.

3. What are you willing to part with? Why or why not?
   Responses you might hear include:
   - Nothing. I need it all.
   - It was my mother's/father's and is very sentimental.
   - I can't get rid of these papers; I might need them someday.
   - I have gained/lost weight, and I need several sizes of clothes just in case.
   - I love my books and do not want to sell them.

4. If I could ask you to fill in the remainder of these phrases, what would you say?
   - I can never find _____.
   - I don't know what do with _____.
   - When I try to get organized, I struggle with _____.
   - What irritates me the most is _____.
   - What consumes most of my time is _____.
   - I feel I never get a chance to _____.
   - It feels like all I ever work on is _____.
   - I'm really concerned about _____.

History of Disorganization

A yes answer to all three indicates the person is chronically disorganized.
1. Have you been disorganized most of your adult life?
2. Does your disorganization affect you every day of your life?
3. Have you tried to get organized before?

Expectations
1. What will "organized" look and feel like to you?
2. What are your expectations of a professional organizer?
3. Do you plan to work with me hands-on or do you prefer to have me work alone and ask you questions as I need to?
4. What must happen for this to be a successful experience for you?

Scheduling the Project

Once you have completed the tour with your client, ask to sit down at a table. Review with your client what you heard them say their goals and vision are for each space and clarify anything you need to. Communicate to your client that you will take all the information gathered and prepare an organizing plan of action, which you will follow in your work together, or a plan for the client if they want to do the work themselves.

If they want to work hands-on with you, ask them to get their calendar. Review how you work with clients—for example, the number of minimum hours. Schedule at least the first two sessions for working on the project. Depending on what the project is, you might want to schedule several days in a row to avoid disruption of the space over a long period of time. Or you might want to schedule standing appointments over the course of time—for example, every Monday from 9 a.m. until noon for four weeks.

If you didn't send your client your fees and services agreement digitally, either by email or through DocuSign, present your services and fees agreement and review it with your client. Then obtain their signature (more information on the services and fee agreement below). If you require prepayment of services, collect your fee now.

Services and Fees Agreement

Your services and fees agreement discussion with your client is part of the needs assessment client phase, and it includes:

- services to be performed
- fees associated with services
- time to perform services
- payment policy
- cancellation policy
- materials
- travel
- product procurement

- limitations of liability
- what you will not provide

Disclaimer: I am not engaged in rendering legal advice or services. Therefore, I highly recommend you work with an attorney to prepare your job agreement, as it will need to be defensible in the state(s) you do business in and by your attorney.

Job Agreement Components (See the Forms Section in Appendix A for an Example of a Services and Fees Letter of Agreement)

- Services to be performed: clearly state what the client can expect from you for each type of service (needs assessment, consultation, hands-on, coaching, maintenance, etc.).
- Time to perform services: clearly state the minimum or maximum amount of time for each type of service (needs assessment, consultation, hands-on, coaching, maintenance, etc.).

What to Say When Asked How Long the Implementation Will Take

- Turn the question around and ask the client how long they think it would take them to complete the project on their own.
- Ask, "Do you have a budget for this project?"
- It's a good idea to know what your client is willing to spend to achieve their goals. If it is less than you think you can work with to complete the project, you can suggest working hands-on with them for X number of hours and then give them assignments to complete the project. Allow for the expense of consultations and follow-up in between assignments.
- Every client and every situation is unique and cannot be compared. Some factors involved in how long it will take are:
   - how difficult it is for the client to make decisions
   - how clearly defined the client's goals are
- Say, "Let's work together for X hours, and that will give me an idea of how we work together and move through the process."
- Remind them they didn't get disorganized overnight. It will take time to get organized and create new habits and behaviors.
- A range of time based on previous experience.

What Not to Say When Asked How Long the Implementation Will Take

- It is not recommended to quote a specific amount of time it will take to complete a project—unless you are very confident in your quote and you are willing to work for less money if it takes more time than you quoted.
- You will be able to better quote your time after you have worked with a client for two to four hours. You will then know how easy or difficult it is for your client to make decisions.

Julie Morgenstern, in her book *Organizing from the Inside Out*, suggests the following time allotments for each step in different areas of a home:

Area	Sort Purge	Assign a Home	Contain & Label	Equalize
Attic	16 hours 3 hours	2 hours	3 hours	5 min daily
Basement	16 hours 3 hours	2 hours	3 hours	5 min daily
Bathroom	3 hours 30 min	15 min	3 hours	5 min daily
Bedrooms	4 hours 1 hour	1 hour	3 hours	10 min daily
Closets	3 hours 1 hour	30 min	3 hours	5 min daily
Garage	16 hours 3 hours	2 hours	3 hours	5 min daily
Home Office	16 hours 3 hours	1 hour	6 hours	15 min daily
Household Hubs	4 hours 4 hours	2 hours	6 hours	15 min daily
Kids' Rooms	12 hours 2 hours	1 hour	4 hours	5 min daily
Kitchens	6 hours 2 hours	1 hour	2 hours	15 min daily
Living Room	5 hours 1 hour	30 min	3 hours	5 min daily

- Fees associated with services: clearly state what your fee is for each type of service (needs assessment, consultation, hands-on, coaching, maintenance, etc.).
    - State that your fees are exclusive of materials and tools.
    - State your fee for travel, if you have one.
- Payment policy: clearly state when payment is due for each service (needs assessment, consultation, hands-on, coaching, maintenance, etc.). From my experience, I suggest you get paid at the conclusion of each session, if not before. You could ask for 50 percent deposit. The deposit will commit your client to the session and will give you assurance of payment.
- Cancellation policy: forty-eight-hour cancellation policy is standard. You need sufficient time to book a cancellation to recoup your billable hours. Be strict and enforce this policy.
- Limitation of liability example: "Client will review all materials XYZ Organizing Company recommends being disposed of by means of recycling, shredding, donation, resale, or any other means agreed to between Client and XYZ Organizing Company. Client agrees that XYZ Organizing Company and its employees are not responsible for any loss of damage caused by Client's failure to carefully review or inspect any disposed of items. Client also agrees that XYZ Organizing Company and its employees are not liable for any loss or damage, including consequential damages, Client sustains as the result of services or advice provided to Client by XYZ Organizing Company, or its employees, under this Agreement, including any loss or damage caused by the negligence or fault of XYZ Organizing Company or its employees."
- What is not included in your services example: "XYZ Company consultants do not provide housecleaning, assembly of furniture, shelving, closet systems, moving of heavy furniture, climbing extension ladders, or any similar type of activities."
- Miscellany example: "This letter of agreement constitutes the understanding of standard XYZ Organizing Company services and fees between the parties. Its terms can be modified only by a written amendment to this agreement, signed by both parties."
- Photographs
    - May we print your before and after pictures for reference materials? Yes/No
    - May we include your before-and-after pictures on our website? Yes/No
    - If yes, may we list your name, or do you prefer anonymity? List/Anonymity
- Client signature and date.
- Company signature and date.

Other Business Policies to Consider and Communicate

- What are your fees for:
    - overtime?
    - leaving early because the client asks to end the session?
    - client tardiness?
- How are you going to handle:
    - post-dated checks?
    - bounced checks?
- Are you going to accept a job out of your normal skill range, for example installing closets or shelving?
- Role boundaries—are you going to:
    - babysit?
    - run errands?
    - care for pets?
    - perform housekeeping services?
    - care for elders?
- You need to understand and consider the legal or liability issues with caring for children, pets, and elders.
- Communicate and know your region's regulations on transporting hazardous waste and whether or not you will provide that service.
- Are you going to provide the service of dropping off discards (trash) and donations?
- What is your policy on discussing the following subjects about either you or your client:
    - family members?
    - sexual preference?
    - marital status?
    - religious or spiritual preference?
    - political affiliations?
    - physical or mental health?

Refer to the Forms section in appendix A for a sample services and fees agreement.

ACTIONS

- ☐ Prepare your needs assessment questionnaire.
- ☐ Draft your services and fees agreement.
- ☐ Email your draft to your attorney for review and input.
- ☐ Write your business policies.

CHAPTER 12

Client Process—Phase 3: Completing the Client Project with the 5 Steps to Organizing® Process

Description: The final phase of the client process is preparing the organizing plan of action and completing the project. The 5 Steps to Organizing process was created in an effort to clearly communicate a consistent methodology of organizing and to transfer organizing skills to my clients. It is a time-tested process that will not only give you a methodology for organizing your clients but will also teach them the skills they need to maintain their organization and systems after you leave. This chapter covers:

- creating an organizing plan of action
- 5 Steps to Organizing process details
- keep-let go criteria for client
- stumbling block excuses
- ten organizing principles to maintain organization

Note: The 5 Steps to Organizing process was created by the author and is a registered trademark of SolutionsForYou, Inc.

Organizing Plan of Action

Now that you have completed your needs assessment, you have a much better idea of how you are going to help your client. One way to communicate how you are going to help is with an organizing plan of action. See the Forms section for the needs assessment questionnaires and organizing plan of action template.

An organizing plan of action may include:
- project timeline

- budget
- summary of each room's purpose(s)
- client's goals
- client's vision
- assignments and procedures
- where to place items
- how and where to contain items
- resources, including how to repurpose existing materials and additional materials needed
- vendors and cost estimate for materials
- how and where to dispose of items
- maintenance plan

The following is an example of a completed organizing plan of action.

Organizing Plan of Action—Example

Date

Client Name
Street Address
City, State, Zip

Re:

Dear Client Name,

I enjoyed talking with you about your home-organizing needs and goals. I congratulate you on taking that first step toward living your life more purposefully and taking control of your surroundings!

Based on the information gathered during our initial consultation, the enclosed plan covers what we identified as your organizing goals and vision for your office and meditation room.

If you have any questions about any assignment or product I have listed, please contact me for further direction. Please call me if you want me to work with you on implementing your plan and to arrange dates and time to begin.

All the best,
Your name
Your title

Office/Meditation Room

Step 1—Strategize

Vision: An organized work space. A calm, peaceful, and inviting space to meditate.

Current State:

Purposes:

- a place to process incoming and outgoing paper information for the household
- a place to store paper information
- a place to meditate
- a safe place to store family photographs until they can be organized
- a place to store craft materials

Goals:

Clear the clutter!
Make the spaces visually appealing, inviting, and functional.

Step 2—Prioritize, Group, and Reduce

Assignments:

1. Remove built-in shelving.
2. Commit a day to emptying the area of its contents, cleaning, and evaluating the space.
3. Move items from other areas to the space you are organizing that also need to be part of the grouping and reducing process.
4. Group all like items together by zones (meditation, office, paper, crafts, family archives).
5. Use boxes with labels "keep" (meditation, office, paper, crafts, family archives), "move to another space," "donate," "trash," or "recycle" to sort the items into.
6. Reduce and let go of (donate, sell, trash) anything that you will not use again because of the following criteria:
    a. You don't like it.
    b. You don't need it in your life today.
    c. It's broken, torn, stained—needs repair that you don't have time for or ability.
    d. You haven't used in over six months (other than memorabilia).
    e. It's a duplicate, and you only *need* one.
    f. See attached list of donation resources for where to give your discards a new home.
7. Move to the appropriate room anything that doesn't pertain to the function and purposes of this space.
    a. Move Christmas decorations to basement.
    b. Move books to art studio.
    c. Move vacuum cleaner.

Step 3—Localize and Assign a Zone

1. Purpose the space by creating a specific zone for each activity (see floor plan).
    a. meditation zone
    b. office zone
    c. family archive storage zone
    d. craft materials storage zone
2. Place only the items needed to support each activity in their appropriate zone in containers that are suitable to the item and space.

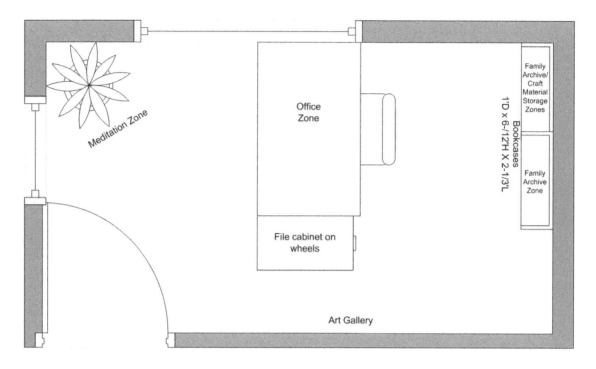

Step 4 —Containerize, Contain, and Label

1. Select containers (see Materials and Resources below for recommendations).
2. Repurpose existing archive storage boxes.
3. Adjust bookcase shelving to the height of storage boxes to maximize space.
4. Install items in containers and label.

Materials to be Repurposed:

- desk: 30"H x 48"L x 30"D (68"L with drop-leaf extension)
- two bookcases: 6½'H x 28"L x 12"D
- two archive storage boxes: 10"H x 15"L x 12"D (tan and green)
- three archive storage boxes: 4"H x 17" L x 12" D (two green / one tan)
- one archive storage box: 8"H x 12½" L x 10½"D (charcoal)
- two wire photo containers: 6"H x 7½"L x 15½"D

Materials and Resources

Item	Purpose	Suggested Supplier	Estimated Cost
Element File Cabinet on Wheels Natural 15"W x 17"D x 27"H	Store household files	Storables	$149

Item	Purpose	Suggested Supplier	Estimated Cost
Archive Storage Boxes	Store family memorabilia	Container Store	$15–$18 each
Archival Storage Box Letter / Legal Size	Store large photos and papers	Container Store	$17 each
Archival Photo Storage Box	Store photos up to 5" x 7"		
Expedit Cube Bookcase	Option for containing craft and family memorabilia	Ikea	$79 each

Step 5— Maximize, Evaluate, and Maintain

1. Is everything as easy as you like it to be?
2. Is the space as you envisioned it in step 1?
3. Do the zones and categories work well for you?
4. Write a maintenance plan.
5. Follow the maintenance plan for three weeks and evaluate where it needs to be adjusted.

5 Steps to Organizing

5 Steps to Organizing®

1. STRATEGIZE

Assess the causes of organizational disorder so that lasting change can be achieved and prepare an organizing plan of action.

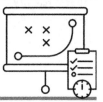

2. PRIORITIZE

Prioritize what to keep by evaluating what items relate to the purpose of the space and what serves a purpose in your life today.

3. LOCALIZE

Assign a specific purpose for each room in your home to eliminate the constant decision-making process of putting things away.

4. CONTAINERIZE

Don't buy containers until you know what you are containing and where you are placing the containers.

5. MAXIMIZE

Organizing is an ongoing process. Write a checklist or maintenance plan for each room.

SolutionsForYou, Inc.
www.solutionsforyou.com

My 5 Steps to Organizing process and principles are based on creating new *habits* and behaviors rather than a one-time clean-sweep event. The change needs to occur *internally* as well as externally for it to be lasting. Identifying your client's current habits is essential to creating new habits and behaviors toward organization.

The 5 Steps to Organizing are intended to be basic and simple. If a process is too complicated, your client will not be able to follow it or learn basic but essential organizing skills.

Step 1— Strategize

Make a plan for your home. This is the first step in the organizing process. Use a spiral notebook to capture thoughts, ideas, and solutions for each room in your home. Assess the causes of disorder so that lasting change can be achieved.

Walk through your home to discover how one room affects another. Rooms in a home must work together in order for an organizing system to be effective and to create flow. Some questions to ask:

- What do you *call* this space?
- What is the *purpose* of this space?
- What *activities* will take place in this space?
- What are your current *habits* with this space?
- Do you have all the items you need to support those activities?
- What is your *vision* for how the space will look, feel, and function?

Step 2—Prioritize

Realize that organizing is not an overnight process. In this step, you are *deciding* what is important to you today.

- Commit a day to emptying the room of its contents, cleaning, and evaluating the space.
- As you empty the space, place like items together (grouping).
- You will need boxes or designated spaces for: keep, donate, shred, trash, sell, and move to another space.
- Relocate (place in a box labeled "move") or let go of ("donate," "sell," "trash") anything that doesn't pertain to the room's function, activities, and purpose.
- With what is left, reduce (prioritize) and let go of ("donate," "sell," "trash") what doesn't serve a purpose in your life today.

You may have difficulty, or work with someone who has difficulty, letting go of certain items. Questions to help aid you through the decision-making process are listed below and can help to clarify what is important and what is no longer important to you (prioritize). Following the keep-let go criteria questions are stumbling block excuses we make for not letting go of an item and responses to help you see a more realistic perspective.

Keep-Let Go Criteria

Practical Questions
1. Is it useful and beautiful to you?
2. Is it a duplicate?
3. Is this the best place for it?
4. If you keep it, will you remember you have it?
5. If you remember you have it, will you be able to find it?
6. How are you going to display it / store it / use it?
7. Do you have room for it?
8. Do you need it or just want it or neither?
9. How long do you need to keep it? When can you let go of it?
10. Is it too worn/broken/unidentifiable?
11. Is the information still current?
12. Will you actually use it / refer to it?
13. When's the last time you used this item?
14. When do you think you will use it again (or for the first time), and what circumstances will have to be in place in order for you to use it?
15. Is this adding value to your life (or home or business) right now?
16. Can it easily be duplicated or created if needed again?
17. What's the worst that can happen if you toss it?
18. Will you really read it? When?
19. Are you really going to finish this quilt (or another project)? When?

For Clothes
20. Do you feel great in it?
21. Does it match anything?
22. Does it fit well?
23. How many do you have of this (i.e., how many white T-shirts do you have)?
24. Is this of high value or importance, or is it getting in the way of your ability to find what you need, when you need it?

Emotional Questions

25. Does it make you happy to see it?
26. Does it make you mad, sad, or feel bad to see it?
27. Does it make others unhappy to see it?
28. Do you love it?
29. Are you honoring and enjoying it?
30. Does it lift your spirits to look at it?
31. Where did it come from / who gave it to you? (Sometimes it turns out to have been a gift from someone they left behind long ago, or just don't like.)
32. Are you keeping it because someone gave it to you and you will feel guilty if you get rid of it?
33. If we took a picture of it, would that make it easier for you to let it go?
34. If you knew (or visualized) that someone else would really benefit from having this (i.e., if we found a great place to donate it), would that make it easier for you to let it go?
35. Convince me that you need to keep it.

When Dealing with Memorabilia

36. Do you have anything else that reminds you of this (event, person, time)?
37. Are you putting things before people and relationships?

Financial/Legal Questions

38. Does it belong to you?
39. Are you legally required to keep it?
40. Would you need this check/document in a legal dispute (i.e., divorce, child custody)?
41. Is there a tax reason to keep it?
42. Will this help you make money?
43. Will this save you money?
44. Would you buy it again?
45. Can you borrow or purchase another one if needed?
46. Does it take more time and effort to manage than it is worth?
47. If you were moving, would you want to pay to have it packed and moved?
48. What does it cost you to keep, store, and maintain it?
49. If you donate it, can you get a deduction?
50. If you sell it, what could you do with the money?

Stumbling Block Excuses

Excuse #1: "I might need it someday."
Look at each item as though you were packing it (or not) for a move. Does the item still have a purpose in your life today? Ask yourself, "If I were to move this item, where would it live in my home?" Why isn't it living there in your current home?

When I hear my client say they might need it someday, I hold up a calendar and say, "I see Sunday, Monday, Tuesday, Wednesday, Thursday, Friday, and Saturday on this calendar. Can you show me someday?" I ask them to physically circle a day on the calendar as someday, and if they haven't used any of the items they designate as "someday" by that date, they need to donate them. Hanging on to stuff you aren't currently using makes it harder to access the things you are using.

Excuse #2: "I don't know what to keep."
This usually relates to paper. The amount of paperwork you receive can cause you to freeze, especially when much of the paperwork seems to be "important." The US Postal Service attests to the fact that contemporary Americans get more mail in one month than their parents did in an entire year, and more mail in one year than their grandparents received in a lifetime. And that doesn't include email! It's no wonder we have difficulty discerning what is important. Essentially, you need to keep paperwork for which you have a purpose. There are five purposes to keep papers: 1) taxes, 2) resale of property/cost basis, 3) agreements you have, 4) certificates/legal proof, and 5) returns (receipts) or disputes (claims). Be clear what that *purpose* is and store the paper so that you can access it when that time comes. Most paper (in fact 80 percent) has no future. Toss it!

Excuse #3: "It was a gift."
Once a gift is given to you, you are free to do with it what you choose. The object isn't the gift. The gift is the act—someone thought of you and wanted to express their thoughts in a tangible object. My mom told me when I was a child, "It's the thought that counts." Think good thoughts. Now get rid of all those gifts you don't use or love. I'm sure you never gave anyone a gift and thought, *I love you very much, and I hope this is a burden to you for the rest of your life!* The love is in the giving. Use it, love it, or give it to someone who can. You have my permission to get rid of any gift you don't use or love.

Excuse #4: "It reminds me of my mother."
People associate an object with a special memory. The object is not the memory; the memory is inside you. Take a picture and let go of the object. To preserve the memory,

write about the memory in a journal and place the picture of the item with your journal entry. There it will be preserved so that you won't forget, and generations after you will have the memory too.

Excuse #5: "I paid a lot of money for it."
The monetary value of any item is only that for which you could sell it. Don't hesitate to part with something simply because you paid a lot of money for it. Keeping items that don't serve a purpose in your life today cost you in terms of lost productivity and sacrifice of freedom. Plus, it is negative energy. It makes you *mad* that you spent a lot of money for something that you are not using anymore, and keeping that item around is a constant reminder of that feeling. For example, many people are transitioning from the big, bulky computer monitor or TV and replacing it with a sleek, slim, and sexy flat-screen monitor. Yet they keep around those hulky monitors because they paid a lot of money for them. One of the criteria I use with clients in helping them to decide whether or not to keep something is that if it makes you feel bad or mad, get rid of it! If you are storing items in an offsite storage unit, consider the cost savings you will have if you no longer need the storage unit.

Excuse #6: "I don't have the time to get organized!"
I would be a very wealthy person if I had fifty dollars for every time I hear this excuse! Granted, our "free time" is precious, and the last thing you want to do is spend your limited free time eliminating the clutter in your life.

But clutter monopolizes our time. How much time do you spend looking for your keys, an unpaid bill, or the permission slip for your kid's field trip? Does watching a favorite DVD involve sorting through your disorganized collection—so you go out and rent a movie you already own? The time you lose because of the clutter is easily doubled when you consider the time, energy, and effort that are sapped from you mentally and psychologically. One effect of clutter is that you shut down. You have to spend all your energy just coping with the mess, rather than tending to the things that really matter to you. No matter how deep the clutter is, you can make the time to free yourself from it. It's an investment in yourself that will turn things around. And after you've made that investment and created new habits with your new systems, the time spent will come back to you with compounded interest!

Step 3—Localize

Assign a specific purpose for each room in your home. This may sound simple, but things become nomadic when there is not a predetermined place to store them.

Knowing the function (purpose) of each room in your home eliminates the constant decision-making process of putting things away.

- Evaluate the desired activities for each room in your home and plan to store the items that support those activities nearby.
- Create specific zones in each room for each activity.
- Place only the items needed to support each activity in their appropriate zone.
- Place the items you need to access frequently in "prime real estate" spaces and items you don't need to access frequently in the other spaces.

Step 4—Containerize

- What items need containers?
- Measure items to be contained.
- Determine where the items will be stored. How many containers can fit and maximize the space.
- Determine number of containers based on volume.
- Decide on container material (wood, metal, plastic, woven).
- Label the containers.

Step 5—Maximize

Organization is an ongoing process. As our lives change, so do our organizing needs. It is imperative to reassess the rooms in your home on a regular basis and make changes when necessary.

Organization is not neatness. In my experience, stress does not come from clutter. It comes from not knowing where to put the clutter away. My home gets messy as my family and I go about living. The difference that organizing makes is that I know where to put the mess away and can have it cleaned up in a short amount of time, without resorting to the shove and close method. That gives me peace of mind.

Ask your client these questions:
- Is the space now as you envisioned in step 1?
- What new habits do you need to create?
- Are the systems working?
- Can you maintain it on a regular basis?
- What will that maintenance plan be?

A maintenance plan addresses what needs to be done and at what frequency—such as daily, weekly, or monthly, as illustrated in this example for maintaining a kitchen pantry:

- Daily keep the zones intact.
- Weekly replenish your pantry with items that have been used.
- Monthly toss expired/stale food items.
- Semiannually reevaluate your zones and adjust accordingly.

Ten Organizing Principles

The following organizing principles are beneficial in maintaining organization and can be incorporated into a client's maintenance plan where suitable:

1. *One in—one out.* When something new comes into your home, something must leave.
2. *Before you buy.* Before you buy an item, decide where it will "live" in your home. If you don't know, don't buy. Go home, look around, and if you can find a place for the item, then you buy it; otherwise you pass on the purchase. Also, consider if you really need the item.
3. *Containers.* Buy containers only when you know what will go in them. Containers are often purchased to "solve an organizing problem," only to create more clutter because the owner doesn't know what to do with them or where to place them.
4. *Label.* Label shelves, containers, drawers, and so on to know where to put away something, and more importantly, so that others you share your home with know where to put away something. A label can be words, pictures, or a combination.
5. *Don't zigzag.* Choose an area to organize and stick with that area. If you find something that belongs in another area of your home, don't move it until you are finished organizing the space you started in. Otherwise you spend too much time moving from room to room relocating stuff, and you lose focus on your original task. Place items to move to another area in a box marked "move." When you are finished with your task, then you can walk around your home and put away the stuff in the "move" box.
6. *Prioritize.* Keeping everything makes nothing important. Decide what is truly important in your life, and that will help you focus on what to keep and honor.

7. *Be decisive.* Clutter is caused by deferred decisions. Don't wait to make a decision about where something belongs; decide immediately and put it there. Return it to its "home" whenever it wanders away.
8. *Set a limit.* Set a limit on how many of something you are going to keep. For example, magazines. Decide to keep one year's worth of each subscription that you will refer to and recycle the rest. Another example is to set a limit on the amount of space you are allocating to a collection.
9. *Paper.* Ask yourself, "Can I get this information somewhere else, such as the internet or the library?" If you can easily access the information somewhere else, you don't need to keep the piece of paper. Toss it! Only 20 percent of what you file for reference you will actually refer to. File wisely!
10. *Maintenance.* Organizing is not a one-time clean-sweep event. Create and follow a maintenance plan for all the areas in your life and home. You can do all the grouping, reducing, and organizing you want, but if you don't learn the skills and follow a plan, you will backslide.

 Exercises

> ✤ Practice the 5 Steps to Organizing process in your environment, with a family member, or with a friend.

CHAPTER 13

Client Follow-Up: Prevent Backsliding

Description: Recognize backsliding and effective ways to address it with a client with these follow-up practices:

- thank-you note
- maintenance plan
- follow-up appointment and evaluation
- client satisfaction survey

Thank-You Note

Do you want your client to remember you long after you have left? Send a thank you note *immediately* after your final implementation appointment. Do you want to make a lasting impression? Send a handwritten thank-you note. Be sure to enclose your business card and before/after pictures! Resources: www.sendoutcards.com or www.organizedgreetings.com. "After" pictures of your client's project are very helpful in preventing backsliding. They give the client a visual of how their space is supposed to look.

Sample Thank-You Note

> Sheila,
>
> I wanted to thank you for the opportunity to work with you. I recognize how difficult it can be to tackle what seems to be an overwhelming project. Working together, I saw your strengths of identifying your needs and staying focused on the vision you had for your room. I also loved the warmth I felt from you, hearing you talk and tell stories of your

grandkids and children. Thank you for sharing that intimacy of your life and family.

I sincerely appreciated you completing my client satisfaction survey and your feedback and your compliments.

Enclosed is an after picture to help you maintain your room.

With gratitude,
Anne

Maintenance Plan

Prepare a written a maintenance plan with your client at your final session. If it is not possible to complete at the final session, include a maintenance plan with your thank-you note.

Include in your maintenance plan the space that needs to be maintained and what in the space needs to be addressed on a daily, weekly, monthly, and quarterly basis.

For example, to maintain a kitchen pantry, your client would need to do the following:

- Daily: keep the zones intact.
- Weekly: replenish your pantry with items that have been used.
- Monthly: toss expired and stale food items.
- Quarterly: reevaluate your zones and adjust accordingly.

Maintenance Plan Template

Area: _____

To maintain this area, you will need to do the following **daily**:

_____
_____
_____

To maintain this area, you will need to do the following **weekly**:

_____
_____
_____

To maintain this area, you will need to do the following **monthly**:

_____
_____
_____

To maintain this area, you will need to do the following **quarterly**:

_____
_____
_____

Follow-Up Appointment

The purpose of a follow-up appointment is to make sure the systems and solutions you and your client implemented are working for them. A client will backslide within thirty days of implementation. Schedule a follow-up appointment within thirty days at the conclusion of the final implementation appointment. Some questions to ask your client are:

- Is everything working the way the client envisioned? If not, what isn't working?
- Have the goals of the client been met?
- Is your client able to follow the maintenance plan?

If the organizing systems you set up are not working, or the client's goals have not been met and they can't follow the maintenance plan, offer suggestions that might help with what isn't working or offer to come back to work together to get things right.

Client Satisfaction Survey

The purpose of a client satisfaction survey is to provide you, the professional organizer, with feedback on your services and meeting the client's expectations. You can include the survey with the thank-you note or as a follow-up email. You could also create the survey with an online tool, such as surveymonkey.com, to collect and analyze your client feedback. Some questions to ask are:

1. Did XYZ Organizing Company provide you with confidential and empathetic advice? If not, please explain.

2. Did XYZ Organizing Company provide you with ideas and solutions, along with hands-on help in organizing chaotic areas? If not, please explain.
3. What ideas or solutions helped you to get organized the most?
4. Do you feel you will be able to maintain the organizing systems XYZ Organizing Company helped you to establish? If not, please explain.
5. Did XYZ Organizing Company meet your expectations? If not, please explain.
6. Did XYZ Organizing Company work within your desired timeline? If not, please explain.
7. Please write a brief client appraisal statement for our records. May we print this statement on our reference listing and on our website? Yes/No
8. If yes, may we list your name, or do you prefer anonymity?
9. Please provide any other comments and suggestions you have for us.
10. Would you be willing to be a reference for XYZ Organizing Company?
11. Would you recommend XYZ Organizing Company to others? If not, please explain.
12. Do you know of others who could benefit from XYZ Organizing Company services? If yes, please provide their name and phone number below.

Actions

☐ Create your client satisfaction survey. You can create it with www.surveymonkey.com.

PART III

Working with Clients

CHAPTER 14

Safety for Professional Organizers and Their Clients

Description: Before working with clients, it is important to understand the potential safety hazards that you might experience. This chapter covers a basic understanding of potential hazards when working with clients, how to increase your personal safety awareness, and insight into how to work safely with your clients and in their environment.

Hazards

Take a look at the picture above of a basement workshop. Think about the hazards you see. What hazards don't you see that might be in this environment? This is an exercise to train your eye to look for safety hazards and make your client aware of them too. When you're conducting a needs assessment with a client, you may get excited thinking about the possibilities of how you can transform an environment for your client, but at the same time, you need to be thinking about what hazards might present themselves during that process. Make note of those hazards and ask your client questions.

Some visible hazards in the photo above are:

- exposed insulation
- a furnace with aerosol paint cans—a highly combustible situation
- a power tool that is plugged in
- cords that can easily cause a person to trip
- lots of sharp tools and objects in this space
- very heavy objects

Some hazards I thought could be present in this environment that I didn't see are asbestos, mold, rodent droppings or rodents, and bugs.

This is just an exercise for you to train your eye and your brain to not only be looking at the possibilities of how you're going to declutter and organize a space but also what safety hazards are going to present themselves to you and your client during that process.

Some potential dangers and hazards are:

- *Aggressive animals.* Even the cutest little dog that can seem quite tame and nonaggressive can turn aggressive if it feels threatened. A colleague of mine had that situation. She was working with a client, and the dogs were just kind of getting under their feet while they were working on organizing the space, so my colleague asked her client to gate the dogs in the kitchen, which the client happily did. Afterward, my colleague realized she had left her work bag in the kitchen. Instead of opening the gate to go into the kitchen, she decided it would just be easier to climb over the gate, which is a bit of a hazard in itself because she could've easily tripped, but she's tall, so she could probably get over it much easier than I could. When she was reaching over with her leg, one of the dogs felt threatened and bit her calf—the back of her leg. So, you want to think about making sure a client's animals are not in the area as you're working, because you never know how they are going to react to your presence or to the process.

- *Back and neck injury from lifting.* This is easy to do in our profession. We are lifting and bending all the time with our clients as we move things around. The best advice is to get proper training on how to lift, using your legs and not your back. Learn how to reach and lift overhead, so you don't injure your shoulders and neck. Most gyms have trainers on staff who can teach you how to lift, reach, and bend properly.
- *Falling down stairs, especially when carrying objects.* This is an experience I had. It's common to be walking up and down stairs in a client's environment, and carrying things in and out, and that's okay; you just need to be aware of when you're walking down stairs even up stairs. You are typically going to hold a box close to your body, rather than extending it away from your body. When you hold it close to your body, you can't see your feet, so it's easy to miss a step—that last step. And if you've ever fallen, missing a step, you know what that feels like. Compound it with carrying a heavy box, and you can injure yourself even more.
- *Falling off a ladder.* I'm not talking about an extension ladder; those you should take precautions with and possibly avoid altogether. But just a step stool—a two-step or four-step step stool—again, it's easy to fall by missing that last step. I was working with a client in her master bedroom closet, and they had tall ceilings in the closet. I could not easily reach the top shelf of the closet with my two-step step stool. My client had a four-step step stool, so we used that instead. I was up and down that step stool all afternoon, and that last time down that step stool, my brain was obviously tired from the work and thought I was on a two-step step stool, and I crashed down to the floor.
- *Tripping.* Tripping is a big hazard and very common, especially to your client because they are used to items being in a certain place in their environment. Suddenly, you're in there working with them, and things are shifting around as you're going through, decluttering and organizing. It is very easy to trip if you're not watching for those changes. It is important for you to be watching out for your client because more than likely, you are the one moving around the objects.
- *Stacked objects falling on you or on your client.* This can happen when working in an environment that has very narrow pathways because there's a lot of clutter stacked one top of another. If you or your client are walking down that narrow

pathway and you bump into the stacked objects, they could come toppling down and cause injury or damage the items.

- *Mold.* Mold is a respiratory concern and can also cause skin infections. You will want to wear a respiratory mask if you are in a mold environment. If you can avoid a mold environment altogether, that's the best. Have someone come in and do that cleanup before you work with your client. If you discover mold while working with your client, wear protective clothing, gloves, and a mask and suggest your client do the same.
- *Dust.* It's common for a cluttered environment to be quite dusty because your client is probably not dusting on a regular basis, if at all. It's not really a hazard or a danger unless you have asthma; then it can be quite uncomfortable in that environment. You will want to protect yourself from breathing in all that dust and causing an asthma attack. Wear a dust mask and carry your inhaler. And wear goggles to protect yourself from airborne dust particles.
- *Heat stroke.* Heat stroke is a potential danger and hazard depending on where you live and how often you have severe temperature conditions. If it is a very hot day, and you are working outside, or in a garage, or even if you are working in an attic where there is little airflow, it is easy to get overheated, which can cause dehydration or exhaustion, and could also lead to heat stroke.
- *Bug bites.* The common ones are fleas and spiders. Some people have allergic reactions to both, and some spider bites are dangerous. You want to be aware of what bugs are present in the environment you're working in and protect yourself accordingly. Bed bugs are becoming more and more common, unfortunately. An adult-size bed bug is about the size, shape, and color of an apple seed. They do not spread disease, but you can have an allergic reaction to their bite. More of a hazard is that you can easily carry them home to your environment. To prevent that from happening, have in your work kit or put on you before you even go to a client site DEET-based insect repellant, because those do repel bed bugs for a few hours. If you are there for a longer period, you will want to somehow reapply the insect repellant. And again, wear head-to-toe clothing to protect yourself.
- *Cockroaches.* Cockroaches, on the other hand, do spread disease. According to Pestworld.org, cockroaches have been implicated in the spread of thirty-three kinds of bacteria, including E. coli and salmonella, six parasitic worms, and more than seven other types of human pathogens. I don't know about you, but my initial reaction when I see a cockroach is to stomp on it with my shoe. That is something you should never do because if you step on a cockroach and it's

pregnant, the eggs will stick to the sole of your shoe, and they could come into your home with you or in your car to hatch.
- *Rodents*. Specifically, deer mice. The concern about rodents is they can cause hantavirus pulmonary syndrome, also known as HPS, which is a severe and sometimes fatal respiratory disease in humans caused by infection with the hantavirus. When fresh rodent urine, droppings, or nesting materials are stirred up, tiny droppings containing the hantavirus get into the air. You can easily breathe that in, and that can cause the severe or fatal respiratory disease. Do not sweep, vacuum, or touch rodents or their droppings. Clients have asked, "Can't we spray down the area? Then it will be wet and won't be airborne." That is not 100 percent secure. The safest approach is to contact a pest control service for removal and handling.
- *Needle sticks*. Those are injectable needles, such as what a diabetic might use to inject insulin into their body. Do not handle them. Ask your client to dispose of them properly. You may say, "Why in the world would I come across needle sticks?" Believe me, I have been in clients' environments where they are not being careful with them. It is very easy to be reaching around and picking things up, and suddenly, you're coming in contact with a needle stick. I suggest you wear protective gloves if you're working in a heavily cluttered environment where you cannot always see what you are reaching for.
- *Compassion fatigue*. Compassion fatigue is due to ongoing exposure to client struggles. New professional organizers are probably not going to experience this, but as time goes on, you might experience compassion fatigue. Compassion fatigue is a specialized form of burnout in which the professional organizer no longer feels able to help their clients. That hopeless feeling might not be conscious to the professional organizer; instead, it might manifest as cynicism, or a growing disdain of clients, or it could be that you experience impatience, an inability to empathize, or overall job dissatisfaction. If you wake up in the morning and are not jumping up and down, all excited to go organize with a client, you might want to stop and think about what is going on. Maybe you are starting to experience compassion fatigue. If you experience these symptoms, a consultation with a trusted peer or mentor can help, and professional counseling should be among the options you consider if you are not able to get back on track on your own.

Safety Points

The safety points below are from Debbie Stanley's book titled *Let Me Show You the Basement*. The title is based on an experience that she had with a client who she names Mr. Creepy.

- Take a self-defense class to prepare you for the event of a personal attack.
- Use a separate phone number for your business.
- Have a post office box for your business address. There's no reason why your clients should be able to have access to you personally by phone or physical address.
- Familiarize yourself with the client's location.
- Have your cell phone turned on, and on your body, not in your work bag.
- Be able to leave your work bag and purse. Whatever you have in your bag or your purse you need to be okay to leave behind should you need to. Be sure your address is not on something you might leave behind.
- Wear clothing and close-toed shoes that you can easily run in should you need to make a hasty retreat.
- Always let someone know where you are. You can do this by sharing your calendar either online or leaving a paper copy at your home office. That's particularly important for professional organizers who live alone. Should you go missing, it is going be very helpful if there is some type of a trail to start with and having your calendar visible and accessible is one way to do that.
- Leave something by the entry door.
- Always walk behind your client and locate exits.
- Do not reveal too much personal information.
- Do not accept food or beverages from clients unless you know and trust them well.
- Carry dog treats to ward off aggressive domestic dogs.
- Do not wear excessive jewelry.
- Consider wearing your hair up if it is long.
- Keep your hands free and above your waist.
- Last, but most importantly, trust your instincts. If you have ever trusted your gut to be a barometer for dangerous situations, then that's something that you should trust in interacting with clients as well. Gavin de Becker, who wrote the book *The Gift of Fear*, says "Intuition is knowing without knowing why." It's that feeling, and if you get that feeling, then it might be best to say no to that particular client opportunity.

Your Client's Safety

Know your and your client's physical limitations when lifting, reaching, bending, and climbing stairs. Don't exceed your limitations, no matter how hard someone pushes, and don't push your client to exceed theirs.

Eat something and take any medications you need before a client session and instruct your client to do the same. Clients always ask, "What should I do to prepare?" One of the tasks I have them do to prepare is to eat something and take their medications before our session.

Every forty-five minutes to an hour, take a break by getting up and stretching. Get something to drink and get some fresh air, and have your client do the same.

Have a first aid kit in your work bag and onsite with you, and you might want to add some of the items to protect you from the hazards I mentioned—such as Benadryl for insect bites if you have allergic reactions. If you have any type of medical condition that requires you to have access to medications, have those in your first aid kit.

Keep the area clear of tripping hazards. I cannot say this enough. I have seen clients trip, and I have tripped. It is so easy to do in the organizing process because things are in motion constantly.

Wear protective clothing. I do not suggest that you show up at a client session all suited up in a hazmat suit when the environment doesn't warrant that. You want to be respectful. If you are dust sensitive, simply inform your client you are going to wear a mask because you are sensitive to dust. And you might offer them a dust mask as well.

Personal Protective Gear

- Disposable shoe covers. In case you do need to stomp on a cockroach!
- A dust mask or higher grade, depending on the environment and the hazards that are presented.
- A flashlight because sometimes you just can't see what is behind things, and a flashlight will illuminate those areas.
- Gloves—latex gloves, as I mentioned. Also have heavier work gloves, such as garden gloves.
- Goggles. It can seem funny having goggles on, but sometimes you get in environments where there is dust flying around that you don't want to get in your eyes.
- Hand sanitizer to help in any situation.

- A hat, such as a baseball cap or something like that, for areas with cobwebs and spiders. When you are in a basement or attic area, you just don't know what's creeping around above your head.
- Most situations that we work in do not warrant a hazmat suit, but sometimes having painter coveralls to slip on to protect your clothing is a good idea.
- Insect repellant that is DEET-based.
- Benadryl, if you might be allergic to insect bites.
- An inhaler if you have asthma.

CHAPTER 15

The Challenging Clients You Will Meet

Description: Challenging can mean so many things—difficulty with focusing, an inability to maintain organizing systems due to mental health conditions such as depression or a hoarding disorder, chronic disorganization, and attention deficit hyperactivity disorder (ADHD). This chapter will prepare you for those more challenging clients with an in-depth look at real client case studies.

For each case study, I will describe:

- the client's background
- the condition of the environment
- techniques used to work with the client
- other techniques for working with these client populations
- resistance from the client
- results
- what I know now and wish I had known then

Case Studies

As you read about these case studies, think about who your ideal client is. Who do you want to work with? How does the assessment of your skills connect with these clients? Do you have the skills and knowledge and compassion to help these types of clients? Is this an area you would like to make your specialty? Which characteristics of a professional organizer will help you in working with these types of clients? Which do you possess?

Go back to chapter 1 and look at those characteristics we discussed that might help you with the clients reviewed in this chapter. Consider your skills and background to evaluate which client base is best for you. You do not have to work with everyone that comes your way. That is a challenging statement when you are first starting out, you don't have a lot of clients, and you want to work. So, you think, *Okay, I'll try that*. But you need to consider your skills, training, and experience and whether or not you are capable of working with these client types. There is an organization called the Institute for Challenging Disorganization, and their website is www.challengingdisorganization.com. They have teleclasses that cover working with these client types and many others.

The clients discussed in this chapter may make your heart sing, or they may make you think, *No way!* And that is okay. Whichever it is, be true to yourself and your client in working with them; otherwise, you are doing both a disservice. Above all else, do no harm.

Please realize not all your clients will be like the ones discussed in this chapter. The purpose of this chapter is to make you aware of these client types.

Angela—Clients with Attention Deficit Disorder (ADHD)

ADHD is caused by a neurobiological difference in the brain, which can interfere with such areas as learning, cognitive and organizational processing, socialization, and general life performance.

Client Background
Angela discovered and communicated to me that she was diagnosed with ADHD when her son was diagnosed with ADHD. When a child has ADHD, one or both of the parents have ADHD. Angela was relieved to find out there is a reason why she is the way she is, and now with medication, she was eager to clear her clutter and set up systems to keep her home organized. Angela contacted me in 2003, my first year in business, and I had no clue how ADHD affects a person's ability to organize.

Condition of the Environment
Level 1 on the Clutter-Hoarding Scale[9]. A beautiful home. Most spaces cluttered. Paper (years of it) was kept in beautiful baskets and bags. Every time the cleaning service came to clean the home, all surfaces were swept of paper into these baskets and bags and then never looked at again.

---

[9] "Institute for Challenging Disorganization Clutter Hoarding Scale," accessed June 12, 2018, http://www.challengingdisorganization.org/resources/clutter-8211-hoarding-scale.

Techniques Used to Work with Angela
We spent several days sorting those years of bags and baskets of paper. Then I set up a prepackaged file system for her and taught her how to use it by filing the papers she kept into the system.

Once we completed that process, I had apparently gained her trust, because she said to me, "Anne, I have a room I would like to show you that I think I want you to help me with."

I said, "Great where is this room?"

She said, "Upstairs. It's the bonus room." For those who are not familiar with a bonus room, for the past two decades or more, American homebuilders have expanded homes from having one- or two-car garages to three or four. Above the garage, they build a huge space and call it the bonus room, meaning the homeowner can use the space however they want. And therein lies the problem; it is an undefined, un-purposed space. The picture below is Angela's bonus room.

I asked Angela what she wanted to do in this space. She gave my question some thought and replied, "Well, I like to decorate the house for the different seasons, so I want to store home décor here. And I like to create memory books and other craft projects. Maybe play the guitar and hang out." Angela defined her space as her "creativity center" to give it purpose to help us determine the criteria for what would stay in the creativity center and what didn't belong there. The technique is defining the purpose of the space and what activities will take place in the space to determine what remains and what is jettisoned.

The next week, we sorted and purged her bonus room based on those activities.

After photo of Angela's bonus room

Other Techniques for Working with ADHD Clients

- Find out how and where clients work the best. ADHD individuals are sometimes distracted by sounds that may not distract others. And others with ADHD do better with music playing while they organize and complete tasks.
- Timers or an alarm clock help ADD clients stay on schedule. Timers also help teach clients how to estimate time—how long tasks take.
- Visuals are usually a must for ADHD clients. Calendars, wipe-and-write boards, Post-It notes, or pictures are a few visuals that create reminders for the client.
- Assist clients in making homes for things where they use them. This way they won't get distracted looking for lost things.

- A key technique I use is to have the client ask questions out loud. Hearing what one needs to do can move the decision-making process along.
- Teach your clients to do one task at a time—no multitasking! Examples of this include collecting trash from all over the house at the same time, or putting all dishes in the dishwasher at one time.

Any Resistance

Not great resistance. Angela wanted to keep more than I recommended—mostly paper, because of fear. But overall, she was highly motivated to clear out the clutter. Once she was on medication for her ADHD, everything became three-dimensional, where before the clutter was wallpaper to her, and she didn't see it.

Results

- She has maintained the space since August 2003.
- She lost fifty pounds as a result of our work together.
- She has taught friends how to set up a paper management system.
- *More* magazine interviewed Angela about the best investment she ever made in her life, which was hiring a professional organizer. A few quotes from the article I would like to highlight are:
  - "'Give me a pile of mail, and you might as well strangle me,' Angela Coel says. At least, that was the old Coel. For years, although she managed to stay ahead of the curve at work, Coel always felt as if her 'tail were on fire.' And when she quit her job to stay at home with her kids, her chronic level of disorganization overwhelmed her."
  - "Then in 2002, Coel was diagnosed with attention deficit disorder, began taking Ritalin, and started looking at things differently. Rather than seeing her problems as a moral failing, she began to view them as practical issues to be fixed. She decided to get help from someone whose skills complemented her own—a professional organizer."

What I Know Now That I Wish I Had Known Then

- How difficult it is for a person with ADHD to get anything done—the daily struggles they have.
- The ADHD client feels tremendous shame because they often hear that they are "lazy," "don't care," and "are slobs." They constantly feel judged.
- The value of coaching, either integrated with the organizing, or one person working with her as an ADHD coach and another as the side-by-side organizer.

Clients with ADHD benefit greatly from coaching to be accountable, stay focused, and receive positive affirmations about their progress.
- An understanding of how to reduce distractions and keep clients focused and activated during the organizing process.
- Medication helps tremendously to "activate" someone with ADHD; otherwise, they know they need to be doing something but can't get started.

Trudy—Chronically Disorganized Clients

Chronic disorganization (CD) is having a history of disorganization in which self-help efforts to change have failed, an undermining of quality of life due to disorganization, and the expectation of future disorganization.

You might be wondering, how do you identify a chronically disorganized client from a situationally disorganized client? You can ask your client these three questions, and if they answer yes, they are CD:

1. Have you been disorganized most of your adult life?
2. Does your disorganization affect you every day of your life?
3. Have you tried to get organized before?

Characteristics of Chronically Disorganized and their Environment

- Accumulations of large quantities of possessions or paper beyond apparent usefulness or pleasure.
- A high degree of difficulty or discomfort letting go of things.
- A wide range of interests, unfinished projects, and incomplete tasks.
- Reliance on visual cues like paper piles or stacks of things as reminders to take action.
- A tendency to be easily distracted or to lose concentration.
- A tendency to lose track of time.

Client Background

Trudy is a highly educated and successful professional. She is married with two children and originally from Norway. In 2004, she approached me after my organizing presentation at an organizing supply store. She introduced herself and said, "I think you might be able to help me." We briefly discussed her desire to get organized and set up an appointment for the following Saturday morning.

The Condition of the Environment
Level 2 on the Clutter-Hoarding Scale due to household functions, including clutter beginning to obstruct living areas; slight congestion of exits, entrances, hallways, and stairs; and inconsistent housekeeping and maintenance. Again, a beautiful home—moderately clean—very cluttered.

Techniques I Used to Work with Trudy

- It was an ongoing process of three-hour sessions every three weeks on Saturday mornings.
- At our first session, Trudy instructed me to sit in the chair in her bedroom while she sorted through her clothes; if she had a question about whether or not to keep something, she would ask me to help her decide. When I left her that day, I thought to myself, *What the heck was that about?* At the time, I was reading the book *Conquering Chronic Disorganization*[10] by Judith Kolberg. Serendipity would have it that evening I read about what I was doing with Trudy that morning. It's called body doubling.
    - "A body double is not an active assistant.
    - "A body double's principal job is to occupy space while the client does organizing chores.
    - "A body double must be quiet and non-distracting.
    - "A body double cannot be judgmental.
    - "A body double must be patient and able to sit still for long periods of time."

Laurene Livesey Park, ICD's certification director, shared with me a similar story about one of her clients. Laurene said, "Body doubling was very effective. The client was not able to stay focused. We would sit in her office while she wrote her articles, and I would *anchor* her to the work. She called me regularly to say, 'I need you to come and sit in the purple chair' (the guest chair in her office). When the phone rang, I would say, 'The machine will pick that up.' When she needed a word looked up, I would do that. She stayed in her chair, on task and writing. We even did it remotely once, with me on speaker phone from my office at home, and her at her computer."

Other Techniques for Working with CD Clients

- CD clients agonize over letting go of paper and things. To speed up the process, do a "rapid fire." Place items on a table surface and have the client quickly (within

---

[10] J. Kolberg, *Conquering Chronic Disorganization* (Decatur: Squall Press, 1998).

a minute or two—and use a timer for visual aid) select what they want to keep. Move those items into a keep area and box or bag the remaining items for disposal.
- Avoid kinetic sympathy by not allowing your client to touch their things during the sorting process. According to Judith Kolberg, "Touching a thing can set off an emotional response for chronically disorganized people. Perhaps the touching of a thing changes a simple act of 'throwing out' into an emotional act of 'letting go.'"
- Another of Judith's methods is the "does this need me method." With each item, have your client ask, "Does this need me?" Remember the question is not *do I need this* but *does this need me*? Just let the client's heart respond with a yes or no. If it does not need the client, place it in an area of disposal. This technique reminds me a bit of the Japanese organizer, Marie Kondo's, method of "Does this spark joy?"

Any Resistance
Tremendous resistance to me touching anything or sorting. After two and a half years, Trudy finally allowed me to sort and organize certain areas. Many items were just boxed and stored for her to "deal with" when we were "done."

Results
We did get her dining room organized, including a custom-built hutch.

We organized her storage rooms after she had an unfortunate sewage backup event that destroyed a lot of what was stored there, and she was devastated about that.

The bedroom (pictured above), however, was an ongoing struggle.

One day, Trudy emailed me to say she had to go out of town on business and would call to reschedule when she returned. She didn't. I called and emailed her, but she never responded.

What I Know Now That I Wish I Had Known Then

- CD clients are social organizers and require a great deal of patience. They need someone with them more for the social aspect than the organizing work. The last few years I worked with Trudy, we would start our sessions by walking with her dog to Starbucks and to catch up. This time often took an hour of our three hours together.
- CD clients don't respond well to traditional organizing practices. You need to be creative with them. Make it a game; instead of picking out what to toss, pick out what to keep (treasure hunt) or the rapid-fire technique.
- I would have changed my expectations earlier. I found it very frustrating for a long time and had to manage my expectations about what we could do together. I worked with this client for three years and probably spent the first two feeling like I was failing. But she was happy with the work we did. I had to learn that I was helping her to get through her day, even if her bedroom was still cluttered.
- I learned to redefine a successful client session based on what the client needed at that moment.

Mary—Clients Who Hoard

The three-part definition of hoarding from Children of Hoarders[11] website defines hoarding as:

1. The acquisition of, and failure to discard, a large number of possessions that appear to be useless or of limited value (Frost and Gross, 1993).
2. Living spaces are cluttered enough that they can't be used for the activities for which they were designed (Frost and Hartl, 1996).
3. Significant distress or impairment in functioning caused by the hoarding.

Signs of Hoarding

- extreme collection and storage of items in the home and the yard

---

[11] Children of Hoarders, accessed 2009, http://childrenofhoarders.com/wordpress/.

- accumulation of combustible materials (newspapers, magazines, and rubbish).
- blocked exits (doors/windows)
- narrow pathways in the home
- rodent or insect infestations
- rotting food or used food containers
- human or animal waste
- long-term neglect of home maintenance
- nonworking utilities, such as heat, running water, sewer, refrigeration

Mary is a client of my colleague, Karen.

Condition of the Environment and Client Background
Mary was well educated, articulate, well dressed, well groomed, and lived in a house that was cluttered but not unmanageable (maybe a Level 3 on the Clutter-Hoarding Scale). She had too many and too much of everything by "normal" standards: six part-time jobs, fifteen file drawers filled with teaching materials, several large stacks of old issues of a local weekly newspaper, at least one large file drawer filled with charitable solicitations, and on and on. In addition to her husband, she had two living sons. A third son had committed suicide several years earlier, which was her explanation for why she couldn't throw out the receipt from when he had his wisdom teeth out almost twenty years earlier.

Techniques Used and Client Resistance
When Mary and Karen discussed the accumulation of newspapers, Mary explained that she needed to go through them all to read the obituaries. She said she would feel terrible if she ran into someone at the grocery store and failed to express condolences. Karen reasoned that some of the papers were three or more years old and she had probably already said hello to those people after the loss of their loved one, but Mary could not be persuaded. She was also unyielding when Karen explained that the newspaper had an online database of obituaries and she could search it for anyone she was concerned about.

Other Techniques for Working with Hoarding Clients

- Work with a team of organizers and mental health professionals who are trained to work with hoarding behaviors.
- Treat clients with respect; look for their strengths and build on those.

- Take photos before, during, and after to track results and to help clients understand how *others* see their space, if permitted.
- Be generous and lavish with your praise of their small successes.
- Be trustworthy. If you say you will not discard items without consulting the client, then follow through on that.
- Help clients establish their saving guidelines based on what they will have to give up by saving something. For example, how long will it take to read through twenty issues of the *New Yorker* and what sacrifices will they make in their time to follow through on that promise?

Results
The stack of newspapers never budged in the time Karen worked with Mary.

What Karen Knows Now That She Wishes She Knew Then
Karen said, although it has been fifteen years since she worked with Mary, she just had an ah-ha moment (what she knows now) about two months ago! Karen said, "Clients sure can stick with you long after you've stopped working with them!"

Karen's ah-ha moment was she realized that the triggering traumatic event of Mary's hoarding behavior was probably her son's suicide. Karen didn't even know of the existence of a hoarding disorder fifteen years ago. And she realized that Mary probably felt more people should have reached out to her. And, in Karen's current opinion, that's why Mary couldn't let go of those unread obituaries and the feeling that she needed to take some action about them, but she was probably avoiding them—afraid of what she might find—at the same time.

Karen shared that when she was working with Mary, she, too, glossed over Mary's son's suicide, thinking it was a painful event in the past that would be too personal for her to discuss with Karen.

If Karen had it to do over today, she thinks she would have tried to get Mary to open up about her ideas of death and grieving—in the context of the newspapers. Maybe Mary would have a breakthrough moment, or maybe they would reach the point where Karen could suggest Mary seek some help and support elsewhere.

Priscilla— Senior Clients

"As the year 2011 began on Jan. 1, the oldest members of the Baby Boom generation celebrated their 65th birthday. In fact, on that day, today, and for every day for the next 19 years, 10,000 baby boomers will reach age 65."[12] And that is just in the United States.

Client Background
In 2012, Priscilla was eighty-six years old, and her husband, Don, was ninety. Don had dementia, and it had progressed to the point where Priscilla was taking care of everything in their 2,000-square-foot home—the housework, their finances, meal planning and preparation, arranging for home repairs and maintenance, yard work, all the driving. Everything! Priscilla also had neuropathy in her feet, causing difficulty walking, and she had experienced a few too many falls. It was time for Priscilla and Don to move to a community where they had freedom from all of the day-to-day chores and upkeep, with onsite care.

They found a wonderful community. But the apartments are tiny (500 square feet). That was when Priscilla contacted me.

She said, "It is one of the moments in your life that you know is coming, but you can quickly get overwhelmed by the thought of doing, downsizing, and moving. Because, before the move, there is the enormous task of going through all of the stuff, stuff, and more stuff."

Priscilla and Don were wildflower and scenic photographers, and they traveled the world for years. You can't even imagine the thousands of slides they accumulated over the decades.

The Condition of the Environment
Level 1 on the Clutter-Hoarding Scale.

Techniques Used to Downsize Priscilla and Don
As with any project that seems overwhelming, it is helpful to break it down into tasks with deadlines. It can help you and your client gain control and feel a sense of calm. I pulled together our project plan and gave Priscilla tasks that she could complete on her own, such as change of address notices, canceling utilities, mail forwarding, changing home insurance, collecting necessary papers/valuables, and so on.

---

[12] Pew Research Center, accessed June 12, 2018, http://www.pewresearch.org/fact-tank/2010/12/29/baby-boomers-retire/.

Priscilla and I went through their entire house and put color "dot" stickers on everything they wanted to take with them. The dots made it very easy when I worked with the movers to pack. If it had a dot, it got packed; if not, it was left behind. It took quite some convincing for Priscilla to not pack up her entire kitchen. I had to remind her one of the reasons for the move was so she wouldn't need to meal plan and cook as much—if at all. The one area she would not downsize was her spices, not even her pumpkin pie spice.

Priscilla wanted some new furniture, and we needed to maximize their small space. We designed a floor plan to determine where and how the existing and new furniture would fit.

We went to Ikea. I thought Priscilla would faint at the enormity of it. Even though we were armed with a plan of what specific items we wanted, we were there three hours. I was exhausted, but not Priscilla! From there, we went to several stores in search of wall-mounted switch lamps—not an easy find these days. We found two at a hardware store. I drove Priscilla home and continued to the Container Store to purchase elfa drawer systems and other organizing products for their downsized space.

Other Techniques for Working with Seniors

- Safety is always the first issue to address with any client, but even more so with the aging population. Help them be safe:
    - Remove trip and fall hazards (clutter, loose rugs, etc.).
    - Suggest use of slip hazards (for example, for getting in and out of the shower).
    - Watch for medication hazards. Help them keep track of what they have taken to avoid over/under dosage.
- Keep things within reach, so they don't have to move anything out of the way.
- Seniors are often concerned about people forgetting them after they are gone. They hold on to their things to represent them after they are gone. A useful technique I apply with seniors who are reluctant to let go of their belongings for fear they (the client) will be forgotten is for them to tell me the story behind their belongings. Remind clients that their legacy comes from more than their possessions. I record their storytelling and take a photograph of the client with the possessions they are letting go of for them to share with their family.
- Affirm clients by treating them and their belongings with the utmost dignity and respect and by acknowledging the legacy they are creating.
- Work on reducing their papers to fit in a single file cabinet or banker's box.

- Set up automatic withdrawals for payments or online bill paying.
- Place their name on the do not mail and do not call lists.
- Use a large font with clear letters so they can see it.
- Simpler is better.
- Suggest assistive devices like grab bars and grab handles.
- For memory challenges, leave notes in visible places.
- Work at the client's pace. Be patient and compassionate.

Resistance from Priscilla
None! Her son kept trying to convince her she needed to keep things she didn't want to. But Priscilla was firm and didn't move anything she had already decided not to pack. Don was very resistant to moving. People with dementia have great difficulty with changing their environment. He was depressed for several months after the move. However, once his new home became familiar to him, the depression lessened.

Results
The weekend of the move, Priscilla and Don stayed with their daughter while my team and I worked with the movers, assembled furniture, installed lamps, shelves, and pullout drawers, got all of their electronics working, and organized their downsized stuff in their new home.

Following the move, we held a two-day estate sale and then had a service come in and take away everything that didn't sell to go for donation or disposal. Next, the housecleaners came and did a thorough cleaning in time for the new homeowners to move in the following day! It all took place over five days!

What I Know Now That I Wish I Had Known Then
I enjoy working with the senior population. Starting out in this profession, I didn't think I would enjoy working with seniors because I didn't feel I could relate to them. With just a few years away from being a senior myself, I find I now relate very well with the senior population and understand their needs and struggles.

The Institute for Challenging Disorganization is a multinational learning community and offers education, research, and strategies covering ADHD, CD, hoarding, aging and other client populations. You can obtain certificates of study and earn five levels of certification. You can learn more at their website, www.challengingdisorganization.org.

I hope Angela, Trudy, Mary, and Priscilla have given you the vision to inspire change in who your ideal client population is and to further your education to service them the very best you can.

CHAPTER 16

Working with Clients on Paper Management

Description: This chapter will teach you techniques and systems for how to work with clients on organizing their household paper information, including:

- benefits of organizing your paper information
- the ART of paper management
- how to create a paper processing center
- where to start
- file strategies
- how to identify what paper to toss and what to keep (and for how long)
- where and how to keep your paper information
- products and systems that can help you organize paper information
- products that can help track finances

Note: The content of this chapter is written for you to communicate to your clients, rather than to you the professional organizer. However, the information may also be of value to you in organizing your own paper documents. The information may be reproduced by you, the professional organizer, to present at workshops.

Benefits of Organizing Your Paper Information

A benefit of organizing your paper is you will know where to look for the information you need for many transactions, such as:

- financial and estate planning
- investment options
- refinancing
- bill paying

- tax preparation
- health records
- educational records
- loans

When your paper is processed, acted on, and stored properly, you are rewarded with the benefits of effective record keeping. You will be able to find the information you need and when you need it. The result is a less cluttered environment and mind, allowing you to focus on your priorities and goals and not piles of paper.

The ART of Paper Management

Information comes to us in many forms but most predominately in paper form. It arrives from snail mail, email, children's backpacks, spouse's briefcases, and many other avenues. We know how we obtain paper information; it's what we do with it after it arrives that many struggle with. The following Paper Information Organizational Chart will help you to picture how to process your paper information so that it goes where it belongs. A matching system should be created for your electronic information. Sort your paper by:

Action
Reference
Toss

Paper Information Organizational Chart

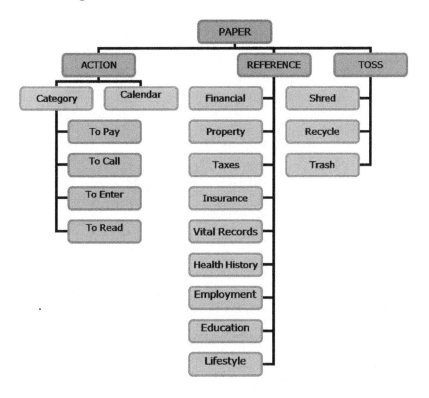

Create a Paper-Processing Center

Assign an area for each activity within the paper-processing center, including an area for:

- action papers
- reference papers to file
- trash
- recycling
- shredder or container for materials to be shredded

Move items needed to support each paper-processing activity to its zone, such as containers for trash, recycling, reference papers to file, action papers, and those to be shredded. Below is a physical office layout of each paper-processing activity zone.

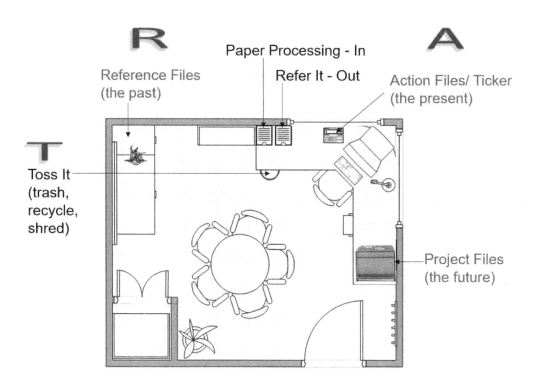

Where to Start

Start with the papers that are your most recent (within the past month). Once you have processed your recent papers, you can address your piles of paper and filed papers in old systems.

File Strategies

The number one question you will hear from clients is, "How do I decide what paper is important and how long do I keep it?" Before deciding whether to keep a piece of paper, you need to decide its purpose. Is it information you will refer to later, or is it something you need to act on? If it is something you will refer to later, do you need to keep the information in paper form or can it be kept electronically? If the paper information is something you are actively working on now, it is considered an "action paper." Action papers will usually sit out on a desk or work space for quick and easy access. If the information is something you will need to refer to later, such as last year's income tax records, warranties, or an insurance contract, put it in a "to file" folder or container to be filed in a reference or archive filing system.

What to Keep and How Long

Each situation is unique. For your financial records, always seek the advice of a CPA for your specific requirements. You do need to keep paperwork for which you have a purpose. Five purposes to keep papers are 1) taxes, 2) resale of property / cost basis, 3) agreements you have, 4) certificates / legal proof, and 5) returns (receipts) or disputes (claims). Some questions to ask to help you decide if you need to keep a piece of paper are:

1. Are you legally required to keep it?
2. Would you need this check/document in a legal dispute (i.e., divorce, child custody)?
3. Is there a tax reason to keep it?
4. Is the information still current?
5. Will you actually refer to it later?
6. When's the last time you used this item?
7. Can it easily be duplicated or created if needed again?
8. What's the worst that can happen if you toss it?
9. Will you really read it? When?

How and Where to Keep the Paper Management System

Choose a labeling system for both your action papers and your reference papers that works best for how the person the file system is being created for thinks about accessing this information.

Action Papers
Keep action files in vertical view on the desk top in a file box. Typical actions are:

- to pay
- to call
- to enter
- to read

Reference Papers
Reference papers belong in a reference filing system in labeled files, by category and alphabetical. Prepackaged file kits can be helpful in determining categories and preparing labels, such as File Solutions Home Filing System (www.filesolutions.com), Freedom Filer (www.freedomfiler.com), and Paper Tiger (www.thepapertiger.com). Depending on volume, store the reference documents in a file cabinet or an archive

file box. Prepare a hanging file folder tab for each **main category** and a manila file folder and label for each **subcategory**. Typical categories or labels for reference/archive papers are:

- finances (credit card statements, bank statements, utility statements, medical payments)
- taxes
- insurance
- personal property (home records, vehicle records)
- vital records (passport, birth certificate, etc.)
- health history
- employment records
- education records
- lifestyle (travel, decorating ideas, pets, recipes, etc.)

Products/Systems for Your Reference Papers—Tax Records

Use one thirteen-pocket accordion file for each tax year and file your paper information in the following categories:

1. Tax filing
2. Financial reports
3. Investment documents
4. Bank statements
5. Credit card year-end summary
6. Income documents
7. Charitable deductions
8. Medical expenses
9. Miscellaneous expenses
10. Child care expenses
11. Business expenses
12. (Empty or for another category you define)
13. (Empty or for another category you define)

Products/Systems for Tracking Your Finances

Use financial software such as Quicken or QuickBooks to:

- Download and track your checking, savings, and credit card accounts—in one place.

- Create and follow a budget.
- Schedule payments and pay bills right from Quicken.
- Verify accuracy of your bank statements and avoid any inappropriate fees or charges.
- Simplify tax preparation, find hidden tax deductions, and transfer information directly to TurboTax software.

Products/Systems for Digital Financial Records

Not all information needs to be kept in paper form. The more paper information you can store in a digital form, the less physical space you will need to store information. One tool that can aid you in storing information digitally is the NeatDesk from www.neatco.com. NeatDesk is a high-speed desktop scanner and digital filing system that scans receipts, business cards, and documents all in one batch. It includes NeatWorks software that identifies and extracts the important information and automatically organizes it for you.

Maintenance—The Key

The key to maintaining organized papers is to *regularly* process papers. To maintain your paper, establish and practice the following routines.

Daily: Open mail and sort. Note any action items in your calendar or on your to-do list. Note any events in your calendar. Shred or recycle any unnecessary mail. File any documents that don't require action in your reference file system. File any action papers in your action paper system.

Daily: review your calendar and update.

Daily: At the end of day, clear your work surface of papers, files, and supplies. Jot down notes with your last thoughts or actions on projects, so you can pick up easily where you left off. Return project and action folders that may have piled up during the day to a vertical system on your work surface if they are still "active." Once "inactive," they should find a place in your reference file system in a file drawer. Put away any materials you've taken out. Returning them to their designated place now will save time when they are needed again.

Daily: Write a to-do list. Make a written plan now for tomorrow. While unfinished tasks, new priorities, and lingering details are still fresh in your mind, write them down. Review your calendar, email messages, and voicemail messages for meetings and appointments that may require prep time. Noting your to-dos on either paper or in an electronic format will keep them handy and easy to find for review and updates the next day. Prioritize your to-dos and schedule them into your calendar *when* you will complete them.

Semimonthly: pay your bills.

Annually: Purge your file system. A good time to do this is after you have prepared your tax filing.

Actions

> ☐ Present a paper management workshop using the material from this chapter.
> ☐ Review and become familiar with the products mentioned in this chapter (www.filesolutions.com, www.fredomfiler.com, www.thepapertiger.com, www.neatco.com, www.quicken.com, and www.quickbooks.com).

CHAPTER 17

Working with Clients on Time Management

Description: This chapter covers how to work with clients to manage their time efficiently, including:

- Identify where your time is spent and discover time robbers through a time-mapping technique.
- Understand what causes procrastination.
- Define your roles and goals for each.
- Create a weekly plan. Learn how to categorize and group activities to effectively manage yourself.
- Identify and choose one time-management system and tool that is right for you and why.

Note: The content of this chapter is written for you to communicate to your clients, rather than to you the professional organizer. However, the information may also be of value to you in managing your own time. The information may be reproduced by you, the professional organizer, to present at workshops.

Where Are You Spending Your Time?

The time map in the Forms section (see appendix A) will give you a clear picture of how you are currently spending your time. It is a great tool to use with clients as well as for your own evaluation. In order to become proactive with your time, you need to know where you are spending your time each day. The most effective way to discover how you are spending your time is to complete a Time Map for at least one week.

How to Use the Time Map

Fill in each one-hour block for one week with general **categories** of activities, such as personal care, opening mail, attending meetings, interruptions, talking on the phone, computer time, specific work activities, family time, travel time, and so on.

The key is to be specific and fill out your Time Map every fifteen minutes or so, noting exactly what just happened. This is similar to a food/exercise log. Document everything you did, including who you talked to and about how long it took. Include:

- each time you pick up the phone to make or receive a call
- interruptions and why
- travel time
- how you feel—whether alert, bored, tired, energetic, and so on
- what your activity **categories** are

At the end of the week:

- Color each **category** a different color to visually see how much time you are spending in each category.
- Search for patterns in not only how you are spending your time but how your time is spent by others.
- Identify your peak energy times and your low energy times.

What Did You Learn?

- What was your biggest surprise?
- What are you most proud of?
- What is something you would like to change?
- What was your biggest time waster?
- What is one thing you would like to have more time for?
- What is one thing you want to spend less time on?
- Do your activities support your goals? If not, which activities do not?

What Causes Procrastination?

If you don't know why you are delaying doing a certain task, ask yourself this simple question, "Why am I putting it off?" You will most likely answer, "Because I don't want (or don't like) to do it." Fair enough. Now ask yourself, "What is it about the task I don't like or want to do?" It most likely falls into one or more of these six barriers:

1. You consider it a low-priority task (when it is not one).

2. You do not have all the information necessary to make a decision.
3. You have not set aside a specific time to do it.
4. The task seems overwhelming.
5. Something keeps you from achieving the task (often the perfectionist need).
6. You do not know what steps to take to achieve the task.

Once you have identified your roadblocks and the steps you need to take, write down those steps and then schedule them in order.

Planning Your Time

Consider what you learned from your Time Map activity as you make a plan for your time. Next ask yourself, "What roles do I play in my life?" For example, my roles are spouse, mother, daughter, sister, business owner, volunteer, friend, and teacher. Using the Weekly Plan handout located in the Forms section, list your roles horizontally at the top of the plan. Underneath each role, write your goals for the week. Now you can schedule your time as you would like to, based upon your priorities. Take some time once a week to plan your week and to evaluate how your schedule is working. Using the Weekly Plan:

- List the tasks associated with each goal. Your tasks can be prioritized with A, B, C, D, or E.
  - **A** = A task that is very important and something *you must* do. You may have more than one A task. You can prioritize these by writing A-1, A-2, and so on. A-1 is your ugliest task!
  - **B** = A task that *you should* do. Reviewing an unimportant phone call or reviewing your email is a B task.
  - **C** = A task that would be *nice* to do but left undone would not produce great consequences, such as phoning a friend or having lunch with a coworker.
  - **D** = A task that you can *delegate* to someone else to free up more time for your A tasks, such as your teenage child doing his laundry instead of you doing it.
  - **E** = An activity that you can *eliminate* altogether, such as watching television.
- Schedule your to-do tasks. The main reason people don't complete their to-do tasks is because they don't plan **when** they will do them.
- Enter your appointments and other commitments in your plan.
- Group like activities together.
- Allow sufficient time for all activities and set limits for each activity.

Time-Management Tools

Your specific tool will help you decide how you can:

- Delegate activities to others.
- Say *no* to other activities.
- Eliminate activities.
- Limit yourself to one method if possible and consolidate all calendars into one.
- Prioritize what must happen each day—high, medium, or low importance.

Choosing the right time-management tool for you is critical to managing and planning your time. There are essentially two choices: paper or electronic.

The pros of a paper planning tool are:

- least expensive
- easiest
- simple
- access anywhere
- won't crash
- multiple sizes
- great overview of schedule (can view month easier than on a smartphone)

The cons of a paper planning tool are:

- space can be limiting
- searching takes longer
- backup requires copying
- if lost, you may not have a backup
- archival takes up physical space
- it is manually time intensive (rewriting to-dos from day to day).

Answer yes or no to each of the following questions. If you answer yes to most of the questions below, a paper planning tool is right for you:

1. I like to see a broad overview of my time, such as a week or month at a glance. Y/ N
2. I am the only one who needs to see my calendar. Y/ N
3. I like the feel of pen to paper, textures, colors, and designs of paper. Y/ N

4. I can remember appointments and tasks when I write them down. Y/ N
5. I like rewriting my tasks. Y/ N
6. I like the act of physically checking off or crossing out my completed tasks. Y/ N
7. Writing helps me think through what I need to do. Y/ N

The pros of an electronic planning tool are:

- portable
- small and hold a lot of information
- can easily move unfinished tasks from day to day without rewriting
- easy to schedule repetitive meetings, reminders, and so on
- can set reminder alarms
- easy to back up
- can serve as a communication tool (email, internet, computer files)

The cons of an electronic planning tool are:

- can view one screen at a time—limited view of schedule
- can crash
- need to keep it charged
- need to synchronize it with computer to avoid overscheduling

Answer yes or no to each of the following questions. If you answer yes to most of the questions below, an electronic planning tool is right for you:

1. I like the combination calendar, tasks, contacts, and phone all in one. Y/ N
2. I consider myself a techno geek, or I like technology and new gadgets. Y/ N
3. I can remember appointments and tasks when I type or key them. Y/ N
4. I like knowing my calendar, contacts, and tasks are backed up. Y/ N
5. I need others to be able to view my calendar and schedule. Y/ N
6. I like alarm reminders. Y/ N
7. I like entering a recurring event once and not writing it over and over. Y/ N

ACTIONS

☐ Present a time-management workshop using the material from this chapter.
☐ Complete the Time Map exercise for one week.

CHAPTER 18

Working with Clients on Clutter Control

Description: This chapter covers how to help your clients deal with clutter by asking simple questions about what they really need and about their relationship with clutter. You will learn how to identify what their stumbling blocks are to letting go, how to move through those blocks to achieve a clutter-free space, and how to create a visual plan of what your client wants the space to look and feel like. You will also learn how to teach your clients to stop cluttering and start organizing, including:

- what clutter is
- why clutter happens
- the costs of clutter
- the benefits of eliminating clutter
- your relationship with clutter
- how to create a visual plan of what you want your space to look and feel like
- how to stop cluttering and start organizing
- the key to staying organized—ten basic organizing principles

Note: The content of this chapter is written for you to communicate to your clients, rather than to you the professional organizer. However, the information may also be of value to you in controlling your own clutter. The information may be reproduced by you, the professional organizer, to present at workshops.

What Is Clutter?

Clutter is anything that *is not* serving a purpose in your life *today*. Clutter is things you do not need, use, or love. Clutter is anything that is unfinished. This usually relates to projects that are started and never finished; memory books and craft projects are typical examples.

Why Does Clutter Happen?

Clutter is caused by deferred decisions. Clutter and procrastination go hand in hand. Look around at your clutter. Most of it occurs because you haven't taken the time to *decide* where it belongs.

What Is Clutter Costing You?

Clutter costs you time, space, money, energy, and relationships. The time it takes you to find what you are looking for because of your clutter. The space you could create for what is truly important to you if it weren't for all of your clutter. The money you spend paying for duplicate items because you can't find what you are looking for—or didn't remember you already own. The energy you expend investing in taking care of all your clutter. The impact your clutter has on your relationships because others don't want to live with your clutter.

Clutter gets in the way of you pursuing any passion or pleasure because you are too busy taking care of and thinking about your clutter. Clutter weighs you down physically, emotionally, and mentally. You need to free up physical space to open up space (physically and mentally) in your life for new relationships and personal pleasures or pursuits. It comes down to this question: do you value your stuff over your relationships, your things over your goals, or your possessions over the vision you have for your life?

What Are the Benefits of Eliminating Clutter?

You will regain what your clutter is costing you: time, space, money, energy, and relationships. You will find what you need when you need it. Your self-confidence will increase as you become more organized. You will want people to visit your home again. You will be able to focus on what is important to you instead of on your clutter.

Why Does Disorganization Happen?

There are two types of disorganization:

1. *Chronic disorganization.* If you have been disorganized your entire adult life, have tried to get organized in the past, and your disorganization affects you every day, you are most likely chronically disorganized. It also means you have not learned organizing skills or systems that work for you.

2. *Situational disorganization.* If you have *not* been disorganized your entire adult life, then usually something happened that caused a change in your life, and your organization systems stopped functioning. This is called situational disorganization. Some possible causes of situational disorganization are:
   - Someone was born, or someone died.
   - You moved or changed jobs.
   - The children moved out or back in.
   - You are getting married or divorced.
   - There is a medical condition or aging issue.

Disorganization is **further** caused by deferred decisions. It occurs because you haven't taken the time to **decide** what your stuff means to you and where it belongs.

Understanding Your Relationship with Your Clutter

Let's take a look at how you relate to your clutter.
Choose from one of the following:

1. Write the story your clutter tells you.
2. Draw the story of your clutter.
3. Take pictures of your clutter.

Next answer these questions:

1. What's working?
2. What's not working?
3. Where are you stuck and why?
4. What is most important for you to accomplish?

Question why and how you accumulate your stuff:

1. Did you inherit it and feel guilty about letting go of it?
2. Do you go to the mall when you feel depressed?
3. Are you addicted to catalogs or online shopping?
4. Other—how do you collect your stuff?

You can choose to stop accumulating more clutter once you understand where it is coming from and why.

How to Create a Visual Plan of What You Want Your Space to Look and Feel Like

Now that you have a picture of where you are at, it is time to develop a plan for where you want to go. Choose from the following:

1. Make a list of the areas of clutter that are driving you crazy and schedule when you will address each area on your calendar.
   1. _____
   2. _____
   3. _____
   4. _____
2. Draw a picture or create a collage of what you want your space to look like.
3. Describe your top three decluttering priorities.
   1. _____
   2. _____
   3. _____
4. Write your vision of what you want your space to look and feel like.

How to Stop Cluttering and Start Organizing

Sometimes just knowing how to **stop** cluttering and where to **start** organizing is the most daunting part of the organizing process. Here are a few rules of thumb to follow when you head down your path to a more organized and clutter-free life:

Begin with Your Biggest Frustration

- Ask yourself what is causing you the most *frequent frustration*; that is where you want to start.
- Is it that pile of paper on top of your kitchen counter?
- Is it your kitchen pantry?
- Is it never finding your keys as you start to head out the door each day?
- Is it your child's, once again, late homework project?

Plan Your Attack

- Plan time for your organizing project. Four-hour blocks work best.
- Have the materials and resources you need on hand (garbage bags, drop box, stickers/labels to identify where items will go, and boxes for sorting).

- Create space to sort your stuff. If you don't have space, rent a Portable on Demand Storage (PODS) unit and sort your stuff in the PODS. Or, weather permitting, set up a space in your yard or driveway with a canopy and some folding tables.
- Don't buy containers until you have sorted and purged your items to know how many you need.
- Arrange with the charity of your choice to pick up your items for donation immediately after your organizing project is completed.

Work with Others and Systematically

- Working with someone can **help you stay focused** and is more energizing and fun.
- Ask a friend to help you get organized and return the same favor or for another trade.
- You may even consider hiring a professional organizer if you feel you need expert solutions and systems.
- Focus on the task; **don't zigzag**! Start working in one area and stick with it until it is finished.

Look out for the stumbling block excuses, and to maintain your newly organized space, follow the ten organizing principles, both discussed in chapter 12.

 EXERCISES

✦ Present a clutter-control workshop using the material from this chapter.

IN SUMMARY

Organizing as a career can be very rewarding and exciting. It requires the best of your creativity and entrepreneurial spirit. The more successful you want to be and the more dedicated you are to accomplishing your goals, the more you will find and work with your ideal clients—providing you with rich experiences.

I am often asked, "Why do you want to work with people and their messes?" I don't think of my clients that way. I see my clients as individuals who have their own unique talents and gifts, and who just never learned organizing skills or have a brain-based condition that makes it difficult for them to organize. It's no wonder; organizing skills are not taught in traditional educational settings. I am constantly amazed and inspired by the transformations my clients go through after working with me and learning how to live a better life—through organization.

My ADHD client Angela is an exciting transformation example I shared with you in chapter 15. Angela was interviewed by *More* magazine to talk about the best investment she ever made in her life, which was hiring a professional organizer. It's a great testament to our industry that someone thought and publicly stated that this was the best investment they ever made. She also lost fifty pounds, a transformation that is not uncommon to my clients. Once clients let go of their clutter, they are ready to let go in other areas of their life.

Another transformation example is my client Patty, who after coaching with me decided to launch her own professional organizing business and attended an Institute for Professional Organizers seminar with me.

There are many client stories like Angela's and Patty's. They are why I work with people to improve their lives through organization. They make my heart sing!

As a business owner, you have to be your own motivator. You need to keep records, keep your marketing materials updated, plan the direction of your business, and stay informed and educated in the professional organizer industry. It can be difficult and require a great deal of self-discipline. But the rewards can far outweigh the hard work and go beyond what you ever imagined possible. Learn from my experiences. It doesn't have to take you two years to get your professional organizing business launched and have a full client load, as it did for me. **Mastering the Business of Organizing** has all of the know-how and tools you need to get your business off the ground and you running with it in no time. Don't wait. Get started now!

APPENDIX A: FORMS

Initial Client Contact Information

Client Name	
Environment	☐ Residential ☐ Home/Small Business ☐ Corporate
Company Name	
Address	
Address 2	
City/State/Zip	
Directions	
Email	
Telephone—Home	
Telephone—Work	
Telephone—Mobile	
Occupation	
Children/Spouse	
Pets	
Budget	
Best Day/Time to Schedule	
First Session Date/Time	
Referred by Or How They Heard About Us	

- ☐ What prompted them to call you?
- ☐ Explain your approach and process.
- ☐ Communicate your rates.
- ☐ Follow up.
- ☐ Email confirmation of appointment and attach PDF of your services and fees agreement.

Intake Conversation Notes:

Onsite Needs Assessment / Consultation Preparation Checklist

- ☐ Enter the appointment in your calendar.
- ☐ Enter the client information in your contacts database.
- ☐ Prepare and take with you a client file, including:
  - ☐ map (directions) to client
  - ☐ Client Needs Assessment Questionnaire
  - ☐ Organizing Plan of Action template
  - ☐ Letter of Agreement (the letter of agreement along with a confirmation of your initial session can be sent via email prior to your session)
  - ☐ invoice for needs assessment (if charging)
- ☐ Take your camera and tape measure.

Onsite Needs Assessment / Consultation Appointment Checklist

- ☐ Ask for permission to take "before" pictures and measure areas to be organized.
- ☐ Complete Client Needs Assessment Questionnaire.
- ☐ Complete Organizing Plan of Action.
- ☐ Have client review and sign Letter of Agreement.
- ☐ Schedule and enter in calendar appointments to complete organizing project.
- ☐ Present invoice and collect payment for services (if charging).
- ☐ Prepare summary of initial consultation—assignments/specific Organizing Plan of Action (at assessment/consultation or following).
- ☐ Send handwritten thank-you note (after assessment/ consultation if no further appointment or after completion of project).

Organizing Appointment Checklist

- ☐ Bring necessary tools, supplies, and products.
- ☐ Take "after" pictures.
- ☐ Present invoice and collect payment for services.
- ☐ Ask client to complete the Client Satisfaction Survey.
- ☐ Schedule a thirty-day *follow-up* phone call _____.
- ☐ Handwritten thank-you note (include before/after pictures).
- ☐ Update your client success stories and reference documents.
- ☐ Update your website.

Residential Needs Assessment Questionnaire

Client Name	

Environmental Questions

1. What specifically is not working for you? (Are you organizing their paper, space, or time?)
2. What is working? (Usually you can find something positive.)
3. What is the function of each space? How would you like each space to function? (List each room they want you to work in.)
4. Is there too much stuff or not enough storage? (Or some combination?)
5. What are you willing to part with? (Ask all family members that will be participating.)
6. Which family members will be working with us? Is everyone agreeable to go through this process?
7. Do you prefer things to be out in view or put away out of sight?
8. What is your vision for this space?
9. What are your goals for this space?

Emotional Questions

If I could ask you to fill in the remainder of these phrases … what would you say?

1. I can never find _____.
2. I don't know what do with _____.
3. When I try to get organized, I struggle with _____.
4. What irritates me the most is _____.
5. What consumes most of my time is _____.
6. I feel I never get a chance to _____.
7. It feels like all I ever work on is _____.
8. I'm really concerned about _____.

History of Disorganization

1. Have you been disorganized most of your adult life?
2. Does your disorganization affect you every day of your life?
3. Have you tried to get organized before?

Expectations

1. What will "organized" look and feel like to you?
2. What are your expectations of a professional organizer?
3. Do you plan to work with me hands-on or do you prefer to have me work alone and ask you questions as I need to?
4. What must happen for this to be a successful experience for you?

Home Office Questions

Electronic Information Management

1. What type of computer do you use?
2. How many computers are in the office? Are they networked?
3. What operating system are you using and what version?
4. Are you proficient with the computer and its programs?
5. Which electronic information manager do you use (i.e., Outlook)?
6. Do you use all the features offered in your program, such as categories?
7. Do you know your email program well?
8. Do you use a PDA (personal digital assistant)?
9. How do you keep track of your contacts?
10. Do you have an electronic file system?

Time Management

1. Do you have a system in place for planning and tracking your goals and objectives?
2. Do you use a calendar or planner?
3. When do you procrastinate?

Paper Management

1. Can you describe the types of information that you are dealing with in general?
2. Describe how mail and other items arrive in your home.
3. Do you have an in/out tray?
4. Do you have a filing system in place?
5. Do you use your filing system?
6. Does it take you longer than normal to gather materials?
7. Do others need to locate information or items in your possession?

Notes

Business Needs Assessment Questionnaire

Client Name	

Environmental Questions

1. What specifically is not working for you? (Are you organizing their paper, space, or time?)
2. What is working? (Usually you can find something positive.)
3. What is the function of each space? How would you like each space to function? (List each room they want you to work in.)
4. Is there too much stuff or not enough storage? (Or some combination?)
5. What are you willing to part with?
6. Do you prefer things to be out in view or put away out of sight?
7. What is your vision for this space?
8. What are your goals for this space?

Organization Structure and Their Job

1. Can you please give me a brief overview of your business and perhaps your organizational structure?
2. Describe for me the type of business activities you are involved in (meetings, presentations, etc.).
3. What happens in a typical day?
4. How many people work at this location?
5. How many people work for you?
6. Do you have a dedicated assistant?
7. Does your business involve travel?
8. Do you have more than one office location?

Electronic Information Management

1. What type of computer do you use?
2. How many computers are in the office? Are they networked?
3. What operating system are you using and what version?
4. Are you proficient with the computer and its programs?
5. Which electronic information manager do you use (i.e., Outlook)?
6. Do you use all the features offered in your program, such as categories?

7. Do you know your email program well?
8. Do you use a PDA (personal digital assistant)?
9. How do you keep track of your contacts?
10. Do you have an electronic file system?

Time Management

1. Do you have a system in place for planning and tracking your goals and objectives?
2. Do you use a calendar or planner?
3. Who else schedules your appointments?
4. When do you procrastinate?
5. How much time do you spend on the telephone each day?

Paper Management

1. Can you describe the types of information that you are dealing with in general?
2. Describe how mail and other items arrive on your desk.
3. Do you have an in/out tray?
4. Do you have a filing system in place?
5. Do you use your filing system?
6. Are there central files that need to be accessed by others?
7. Do you handle your filing or does someone else?
8. Does it take you longer than normal to gather materials?
9. Do others need to locate information or items in your possession, such as files?

Emotional Questions

If I could ask you to fill in the remainder of these phrases, what would you say?

1. I can never find _____.
2. I don't know what do with _____.
3. When I try to get organized, I struggle with _____.
4. What irritates me the most is _____.
5. What consumes most of my time is _____.
6. I feel I never get a chance to _____.
7. It feels like all I ever work on is _____.
8. I'm really concerned about _____.

History of Disorganization

1. Have you been disorganized most of your adult life?
2. Does your disorganization affect you every day of your life?
3. Have you tried to get organized before?

Expectations

1. What will "organized" look and feel like to you?
2. What are your expectations of a professional organizer?
3. Do you plan to work with me hands-on or do you prefer to have me work alone and ask you questions as I need to?
4. What must happen for this to be a successful experience for you?

Notes

Organizing Plan of Action

Client's Name:
Date:
Budget:
Timeline:

Room:
Purposes:
1.
2.
3.
4.
5.
Goals:
Ideas for Space:
Assignments:

What materials are currently on hand?

Recommended Materials Needed to Complete Project			
Item	Purpose	Suggested Source	Estimated Cost

Floor Plan

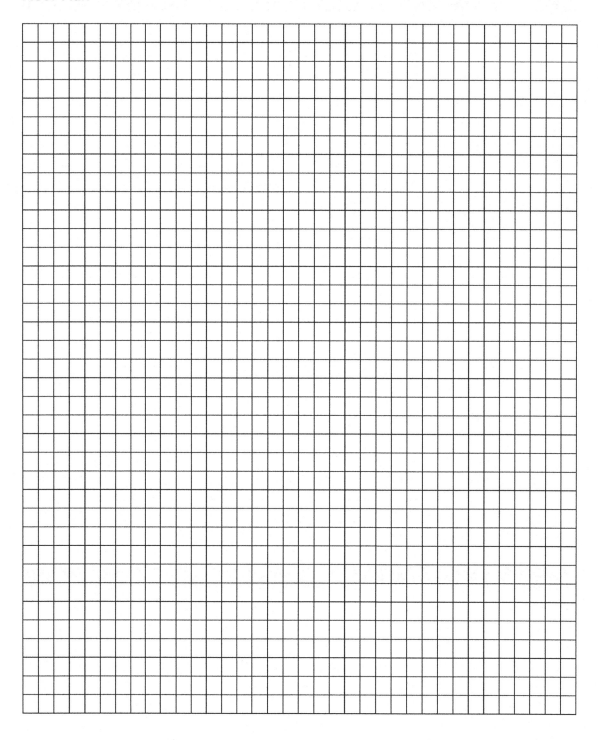

**Example Organizing Company Services and Fees
Letter of Agreement**

The purpose of this Letter of Agreement is to confirm the standard XYZ Organizing Company organizing services and fees.

Services

As a full-service organizing consultant, XYZ Organizing Company will provide the following organizing services based on your needs.

Initial Consultation and Needs Assessment

- Time: *Minimum time is XX hour(s).*

The purpose of the initial consultation and needs assessment is to identify and define the client's organizing challenges and goals. Since each person's situation is unique, it is critical to get a clear picture of where you are and where you are headed before taking one step forward. The initial consultation takes approximately one hour and involves completing a Client Needs Assessment Questionnaire. In addition to completing the Client Needs Assessment Questionnaire, XYZ Organizing Company will measure and photograph the space to be organized to assist in the implementation process.

Implementation

- Time: Varies based on client needs, goals, and participation in the organizing process.

Follow-Up and Evaluation

- Time: XX minutes

Once an organizing system is in place and the client has an opportunity to "test" the system, it is important to **evaluate how the system is working**. Within thirty days of implementation, XYZ Organizing Company will provide a thirty-minute follow-up and evaluation session.

Photographs

- May we print your before and after pictures for reference materials? Yes/No
- May we include your before and after pictures on our website? Yes/No
- If yes, may we list your name, or do you prefer anonymity? List/Anonymity

Exclusions: XYZ Organizing Company Professional Organizing Consultants *do not* provide housecleaning, assembly of furniture, shelving, closet systems, moving of heavy furniture, climbing extension ladders, or any similar type of activities.

Fees

Fee Schedule: XYZ Organizing Company organizing services fees (*excluding materials and tools*) are:

Monday–Friday	9:00 a.m. –5:00 p.m.	$XX.XX per hour
Monday–Friday	5:00 p.m.–8:00 p.m.	$XX.XX per hour
Saturday–Sunday	9:00 a.m. –5:00 p.m.	$XX.XX per hour

Initial Consultation and Needs Assessment fee is due and payable at the end of the consultation.

Implementation fee is due and payable at the conclusion of each appointment.

Follow-up fee: no charge for the first thirty minutes. After thirty minutes, the fee is per the above fee schedule and payable at the conclusion of each appointment.

Travel time over 60 minutes roundtrip is $X.XX per minute and is due and payable at the conclusion of each appointment.

Cancellation Policy: Any appointments cancelled by client with less than ____ hour's notice to XYZ Organizing Company will be charged for the full amount of the scheduled appointment time.

Limitation of Liability: Client will review all materials XYZ Organizing Company recommends be disposed of by means of recycling, shredding, donation, resale, or any other means agreed to between Client and XYZ Organizing Company. Client agrees that XYZ Organizing Company and its employees are not responsible for any loss of damage caused by Client's failure to carefully review or inspect any disposed items. Client also agrees that XYZ Organizing Company and its employees are not liable for any loss or damage, including consequential damages, Client sustains as the result of services or advice provided to Client by XYZ Organizing Company, or its employees, under this Agreement, including any loss or damage caused by the negligence or fault of XYZ Organizing Company or its employees.

This letter of agreement constitutes the understanding of standard XYZ Organizing Company organizing services and fees between the parties; its terms can be modified only by a written amendment to this agreement, signed by both parties.

Signature _____ Date: _____

_____, Client
(print or type name)

Signature_____ Date: _____
Professional Organizer's Name, XYZ Organizing Company

Time Map / Weekly Plan

Weekly Plan

ROLE	Goal	Goal	Goal	Goal	Goal	Goal	ROLE	Task	Task	Task	Task	Task	Task	Task

Weekly Plan

	Monday	Tuesday	Wednesday	Thursday	Friday	Saturday	Sunday
7:00 AM							
7:30 AM							
8:00 AM							
8:30 AM							
9:00 AM							
9:30 AM							
10:00 AM							
10:30 AM							
11:00 AM							
11:30 AM							
12:00 PM							
12:30 PM							
1:00 PM							
1:30 PM							
2:00 PM							
2:30 PM							
3:00 PM							
3:30 PM							
4:00 PM							
4:30 PM							
5:00 PM							
5:30 PM							
6:00 PM							

APPENDIX B: RECOMMENDED READING

Organizing

Author	Title
Jeffrey Freed	*4 Weeks to an Organized Life with AD/HD*
Joan Shapiro	
Judith Kolberg	*ADD-Friendly Ways to Organize Your Life*
Kathleen Nadeau, PhD	
David E. Tolin, PhD	*Buried in Treasures*
Randy O. Frost	
Gail Sheketee	
Judith Kolberg	*Conquering Chronic Disorganization*
Geralin Thomas	*From Hoarding to Hope*
Sari Solden	*Journeys through ADDulthood*
Peter Walsh	*Let It Go: Downsizing Your Way to a Richer, Happier Life*
Sue Fay West, CPO-CD	*Organize for a Fresh Start: Embrace Your Next Chapter in Life*
Julie Morgenstern	*Organizing from the Inside Out*
Susan Pinsky	*Organizing Solutions for People with ADD*
Institute for Challenging Disorganization, edited by Kate Varness, CPO-CD, MA	*The ICD Guide to Challenging Disorganization for Professional Organizers*
Institute for Challenging Disorganization, edited by Phyllis Flood Knerr, CPO-CD	*The ICD Guide to Collaborating with Professional Organizers*
Linda Samuels, CPO-CD	*The Other Side of Organized*
Julie Morgenstern	*When Organizing Isn't Enough SHED*

Small Business

Author	Title
Anthony Mancuso, attorney	*Corporate Records Handbook, The Meetings, Minutes and Resolutions*
Sally Allen	*Independent Contractor Guidebook*
Seth Godin	*Purple Cow*
Consumer Dummies	*Small Business Marketing Strategies All-In-One for Dummies*
Michael E. Gerber	*The E Myth, The E Myth Revisited*
Jim Horan	*The One Page Business Plan for the Creative Entrepreneur*
Anthony Mancuso, attorney	*Your Limited Liability Company: An Operating Manual*

Time Management and Productivity

Author	Title
Brian Tracy	*Eat That Frog!*
David Allen	*Making It All Work*
Julie Morgenstern	*Never Check E-mail in the Morning*
Casey Moore, CPO	*Stop Organizing Start Producing*

Organizing Fiction

Author	Title
Valentina Sgro	*Heart of a Hoarder*

APPENDIX C: WEBSITES

- **Institute for Professional Organizers**
  http://www.instituteprofessionalorganizers.com
- **Institute for Professional Organizers—Training Program for New Professional Organizers**
  http://www.instituteprofessionalorganizers.com/html/certified.html
- **Institute for Professional Organizers—Residential Organizing: A Strategy for Every Room in the House**
  http://www.instituteprofessionalorganizers.com/html/continuing_education.html
- **Institute for Professional Organizers—Professional Organizing Business Forms**
  http://www.instituteprofessionalorganizers.com/html/business_forms.html
- **Coach Approach for Organizers Training** with Denslow Brown
  http://www.coachapproachfororganizers.com/
- **Virtual Organizing Training** with Sheila Delson
  http://freedomainconcepts.com/virtual-organizing-training/

APPENDIX D: ORGANIZING PRODUCTS

My Top Twenty-Five Organizing Product Vendors
(in alphabetical order)

1. **Busy Body Books** www.busybodybooks.com (calendars, planners, and more)
2. **Cozi** www.cozi.com (family calendar)
3. **Dial Industries** www.dialind.com (various organizing products)
4. **Freedom Filer** www.freedomfiler (filing system)
5. **Ikea** www.ikea.com (inexpensive organizing products /furniture/ housewares)
6. **Levenger** www.levenger.com (paper organization)
7. **Living Cookbook** www.livingcookbook.com (recipes)
8. **Mom Agenda** www.momagenda.com (planners, wall calendars)
9. **Neat** www.neat.com (scanner)
10. **Office Max** www.officemax.com (office products)
11. **Org Home** www.orghome.com (storage systems)
12. **Organized A to Z** www.organizedatoz.com (various organizing products)
13. **Planner Pads** www.plannerpads.com (planner)
14. **Rev-a-Shelf** www.rev-a-shelf.com (shelving organization)
15. **Rubbermaid** www.rubbermaid.com (home organization products and solutions)
16. **See Jane Work** www.seejanework.com (fun paper and organizing products)
17. **Smead** www.smead.com (filing products and solutions)
18. **Snapfish** www.snapfish.com (photo organization)
19. **Stacks and Stacks** www.stacksandstacks.com (various organizing products)
20. **Storables** www.storables.com (various organizing products, closets, shelving)
21. **The Container Store** www.containerstore.com (various organizing products, closets, shelving)
22. **Tie Office Mates** www.tieofficemates.com (transparent industrial envelopes and job jackets)
23. **Ultimate Office** www.ultimateffice.com (office and paper organizing products)
24. **University Products** www.universityproducts.com (archival storage)
25. **West Elm** www.westelm.com (decorative and stylish organizing products)

ABOUT THE AUTHOR

Anne Blumer, CPO, is the owner and founder of SolutionsForYou, Inc., a company based in Portland, Oregon, offering professional organizing services to corporate, home-based business, residential, and small-business clients and delivering training programs for professional organizers.

Through the Institute for Professional Organizers, a division of SolutionsForYou, Inc., Anne has trained hundreds of new professional organizers how to plan, launch, manage, grow, and leverage a profitable business. Anne has extensive experience developing training materials and training professionals in the areas of small-business administration and management, employee benefits, information systems, and mergers and acquisitions. Her experience as a business owner and founder of SolutionsForYou, Inc. Organizing Services has given her skills, knowledge, and the ability to provide complete and comprehensive training for individuals.

Anne is among the inaugural two hundred professional organizers in the world to receive the Certified Professional Organizer CPO designation from the Board of Certification for Professional Organizers (BCPO). Additionally, Anne holds a certificate of training from the Coach Approach for Organizers and from the ICD a Level II ADD Specialist Certificate, Level II Chronic Disorganization Specialist Certificate, Certificate of Study in Learning Styles and Modalities, Certificate of Study in Chronic Disorganization, Certificate of Study in Basic ADD Issues with the CD Client, and Certificate of Study in CD Client Administration.

After thirteen years as a work-life benefits manager for a high-technology company and seventeen additional years of administrative and managerial positions, Anne launched her career in the professional organizer field.

> I became a professional organizer because I discovered that what I loved about all the jobs I previously held was organizing my work environment, projects, and tasks. I also enjoyed helping and teaching my coworkers how to organize their workspace, tasks, and schedules. I feel very fortunate to say I love what I do!

With her years of managerial experience, she understands the organizational skills needed to be a professional in today's competitive business place. As a mother of two children, she also knows firsthand what it takes to organize a busy family and keep a household running smoothly. With this understanding, Anne teaches her clients how to achieve work-life balance through organization, habits, and routines.

Anne is a Golden Circle member of the National Association of Productivity & Organizing Professionals (NAPO), the Oregon chapter of NAPO, the Institute for Challenging Disorganization (ICD), and the National Association of Senior Move Managers (NASSM).

As a leader in the professional organizing industry, Anne served on the NAPO Oregon Board 2003–2009 and is a past president. She served as treasurer of ICD's Board 2014–2017. Anne served as NAPO's Education Executive Committee quality assurance director in 2009.

Anne is the recipient of NAPO Oregon's 2009 President's Award.

Anne has a bachelor's degree in organizational communication from Marylhurst University in Oregon.

Anne enjoys speaking to a variety of audiences on the benefits of organizing and is an acclaimed international keynote speaker.